Colet Library No. 11

THE OLD TESTAMENT

" In this lytel boke I praye God all may be to
His honour, and to the erudicyon and profit
of my countremen."

From the *Proheme to Dean Colet's
Accidence* for the use of his " new
schole of Pawles."

THE COLET LIBRARY OF MODERN CHRISTIAN THOUGHT AND TEACHING
Editor: Very Rev. W. R. MATTHEWS, K.C.V.O., D.D., *Dean of St. Paul's*

Other titles in preparation.

The Colet Library of
Modern Christian Thought and Teaching

THE OLD TESTAMENT:
A CONSPECTUS

by

THEODORE H. ROBINSON,
LITT.D., D.D.

Gerald Duckworth & Co. Ltd.
3 Henrietta St., London, W.C.2

First published 1953

Made and printed in Great Britain by
Bristol Typesetting Company, Bristol

CONTENTS

AUTHOR'S NOTE

In sending out this little book I must record my gratitude to a number of people who have helped me, directly and indirectly, scholars, friends, colleagues, old students. My thanks are especially due to two of them. First to my wife who has given me invaluable help in the reading of the proofs. In the second place to the Rev. Canon T. Tatlow, whose suggestions have made the Bibliography possible. Further, I cannot leave unrecognised the kindness, patience and courtesy of the Publishers.

THEODORE H. ROBINSON.

Ealing,
January, 1953.

CHAPTER I

THE OLD TESTAMENT

THE Old Testament is the first part of the Christian Bible. Properly speaking, it is not a book, but a collection of books. We now count thirty-nine, but in three cases (Samuel, Kings, Chronicles) the books are divided into two, so that the actual number is thirty-six. They are of very different kinds. Included among them we have books of history, law, poetry and prophecy. All, however, have been preserved with a definite purpose. That is not to give us information on matters of science, or even of history, though large sections of the books do offer us reliable accounts of events which happened in the distant past. Nor is it merely to delight us with the beauty of great literature, though the Bible includes some of the finest pieces of writing that the world has ever seen; the prose narratives of the historical books, simple as they are, stand out among the world's records for their straightforward and fascinating style. Only Homer could tell a story in so interesting a fashion, and we can see much of the greatness of Hebrew prose even through the old-fashioned language of the official English versions. There are few pieces of rhetoric which can be compared with some of the speeches in which the prophets and others expressed their thoughts. Many of the prophets, too, spoke in poetry of unusual beauty and power, while some of the Psalms reach the highest level, and no poem in any other literature is to be compared with the Book of Job.

Nor is it the primary purpose of the Old Testament to offer us a guide to right living, though this is one of its most important subsidiary aims. We all recognise that the Ten Commandments supply us with simple rules of conduct, or at least with a list of the more serious offences against which we have to be on our guard. In the prophets we have the principles of social life laid down with a sharp clarity which later economists and moralists have never surpassed. Taking the Old Testament as a whole, we may safely say man has never had a better guide to personal and social ethics, illustrated as this is from actual biography and history. But the Bible has more than this to give.

The essential purpose of the Old Testament, and, indeed, of the whole Bible, is to tell us of God and of His dealings with men. These are illustrated from the traditions and history of a particular people, insignificant in every other way, but unique in the influence they have exerted on religion. There have been outstanding figures in the spiritual life of the world, men who have founded new and great religions. There are similar personalities in the Old Testament, but there the real medium of divine communication is not the great individual, but the people as a whole. For Christians there is also the fact that Jesus was one of that people through whom the Old Testament came. He was brought up in its traditions and religious ideas, accepting those which are of eternal and universal value and rejecting those which were merely of temporary or national importance. The Old Testament gives a picture of the preparation for Christ, and in the New Testament much is taken for granted which could not have been assumed anywhere else in the world. The Old Testament is incomplete without the New, but it is also true that the New Testament is often unintelligible without the Old.

It is possible to appreciate some of the Old Testament message through a simple reading of the text as it stands in the English versions. But there is much else, perhaps the greater part, which needs closer and more detailed study. It goes without saying that no literature can be completely represented in translation, and the most accurate rendering possible still makes a good deal of explanation necessary. This, however, is not the only difficulty we have to face. We may safely assume that whatever God has to say to men will be said in the speech and idiom of their own time and conditions. The character and mental constitution of the writer himself has also to be taken into account, if we can get any information about him apart from his writings. There is reason to believe, too, that some of the books have a long history behind them; such a collection as that which we find in the Book of Psalms obviously includes pieces from different periods in Israel's history. People change in course of time; their ideas are modified and their approach to life alters. Now there are wide differences of opinion as to the actual dates at which some parts of the Old Testament were written, but it would be generally agreed that the earliest parts are separated from the latest by an interval of about a thousand years. It is as if we had bound up in a single volume materials which were drawn partly from Saxon England and partly from our own time, with selections from many intervening periods. True, it seems that the language was brought up to date, to a large extent, though in many places we find an old-fashioned style and vocabulary; while in others we have words and grammatical forms which must belong to a comparatively late age.

There are, then, three points on which we have to make up our minds if we are to allow for the temporal and local elements in the Old Testament. These are: (i) the structure, (ii) the date, (iii) the authorship of the different parts. Of the three, the first is the simplest, for we have the material before us in the actual words of the Old Testament, and we can use that with some assurance. Though different people may reach different conclusions, there is no uncertainty as to the material. Dates are less easy to determine, mainly because we have comparatively few external events with which to compare the Biblical material. In parts of the historical books we can refer to the records kept year by year in Assyria and Babylonia, and in one case we seem to have an astronomical reference which would be absolutely certain if we were quite sure that the passage in question does imply an actual eclipse of the sun. But for much else we have to rely on our impressions of the language and thought in which a particular truth is expressed.

We had better begin studying the structure of the Old Testament by looking at the form in which we now have it. At once we are struck by the fact that we have, not one form, but two. In fact, two traditions are represented. One is the Jewish, and the other the Christian. The Jewish Bible had a long history. Most of the books had been long in existence before they were recognised as being divinely inspired, or, to use the technical term, "canonical." There were three stages in the process of building up the Bible as the Jews handed it down to us. The first section to reach the rank of Scripture was the Law, the books from Genesis to Deuteronomy. Next came the Prophets, a term which included more than it suggests to us. There were two sections of the Prophets, the Former, consisting of Joshua, Judges, Samuel and Kings, and the Latter: Isaiah, Jeremiah, Ezekiel, and the Twelve—what we call the "Minor" Prophets. Daniel, by the way, was not included at this stage. This second group, or "Canon," was complete by the beginning of the second century, B.C. In the third " Canon " we find all the other books of the Old Testament : Psalms, Job, Proverbs, the " Five Rolls " (Ruth, Song of Solomon, Ecclesiastes, Lamentations, and Esther), Daniel, Ezra, Nehemiah, Chronicles. It seems that the list was not complete until the end of the first century A.D., and there are still slight variations in the order of the Five Rolls, but otherwise the arrangement is that of our printed Hebrew Bibles. The text was copied again and again, with the utmost care, especially in the Law, and the old copies show only the slightest variations. Even the newly discovered Dead Sea scrolls whose date appears to be somewhere between 150 B.C. and A.D. 250, have comparatively few divergences from the traditional form, commonly known as the " Massoretic Text." These scrolls are probably at least seven centuries earlier than the oldest Hebrew copies previously known, and the close similarity between the texts is a fine testimony to the care taken by successive generations of scribes. This is the more remarkable since Hebrew fell out of popular use after the return from the captivity in the late sixth century B.C., and was superseded by Aramaic, a language belonging to the same general group as Hebrew, and related to it much as English is to German. Parts of Daniel and Ezra are written in Aramaic, and also a single verse in Jeremiah. It was the language normally spoken by Jesus and His disciples ; Hebrew remained a learned study, and was used by Jews in much the same way as Latin was employed all over Europe in the Middle Ages.

The history of the Christian Bible is a little more complicated. Early in the fourth century B.C. Alexander the Great transported large numbers of Jews to his new city of Alexandria. There the normal speech was Greek, and in a few generations the great mass of Jews forgot their Hebrew. They had their sacred books with them, but only a few learned people could understand them. So they were translated into Greek, legend says by seventy learned men. Hence the translation is commonly known as the " Septuagint," and is indicated as LXX. The Law was translated in the middle of the third century B.C., and other portions followed. In the two later Canons it seems that the copying of Hebrew in Egypt and Palestine was by no means so careful as it became in later centuries, and there are often wide divergences. Some of these may be due to errors in copying the Greek text, but others clearly go back to differences in the two Hebrew traditions, and it is not the least part of the Old Testament specialists' work to determine, so far as they may, which text is more likely to have been original, i.e. earlier than the divergence of the two in or after the fourth century B.C.

Jewish Christianity did not long maintain its separate existence and seems to have made little use even of the Hebrew Bible. Except to the north-east of Palestine, all the early Christian Churches appear to have been familiar with Greek; they were formed, for the most part, of converts from Paganism, not from Judaism. So they naturally adopted the Greek Old Testament. But by this time a number of other books had been added. Some of these were translations from Hebrew, others were written originally in Greek. In one case (Ecclesiasticus) manuscripts of a Hebrew text have survived, though it is not certain that this is the form from which the Greek was translated. The Orthodox Eastern Church and the Roman Catholics still keep these books in their Bible, though the Protestant Churches have gone back to the Hebrew Canon, while retaining the Greek order. The Church of England still reads them in public worship, though it does not allow them to be used to establish any doctrine; in other words they stand on a rather lower level than the Hebrew Old Testament. These extra books are called the Apocrypha, and, when printed in English Bibles, are placed at the end of the Old Testament. In this book, however, we are not concerned with them.

For the convenience of readers using the English Bible, we shall follow the Hebrew order, generally speaking. This will give us the oldest organised arrangement, for, as we have seen, it goes back to a time when the Greek version itself was far from being complete. It would be well if this order could be adopted in our normal English Bibles, but the Greek tradition is too old and too strong to be disregarded.

CHAPTER II

THE LAW. 1

THE first five books of the Old Testament are those to which the Jews gave the name " The Law," or, sometimes, " The

Five Fifths." They are traditionally ascribed to Moses, and until after the middle of the eighteenth century his authorship was almost universally accepted by Christians. Jesus Himself always spoke as if He, too, had no wish to dispute the tradition, though He did feel free to challenge and supersede some of the provisions in the Law.

The first of the five books, **Genesis,** may be regarded as an introduction to the other four. It consists of narratives dealing with the nomad ancestors of Israel, leading up to the time when they took up their residence in Egypt. The way is thus prepared for the Exodus, with which the political and religious history of the nation really begins.

The Book of **Exodus** gives an account of the escape of Israel from Egypt under the leadership of Moses, and of their journey to Sinai, where the national life was inaugurated in a great Covenant. A code of secular law is given in detail, and the latter part of the book contains an elaborate description of the sacred tent which is to be regarded as the dwelling of God during the nomad period of Israel's existence.

Leviticus is an extensive code of religious law, giving details of sacrifice and other matters which directly affect the ritual and general religious condition of the people.

Numbers continues the story of Israel's experiences in the nomad period, and includes also a certain amount of religious law, with occasional examples of the way in which it worked.

Deuteronomy is largely a recapitulation of the code already found in Exodus. It is expanded, both in specific laws and by the addition of further regulations. It is introduced by a brief resumé of Israel's life as a nomad people, together with earnest exhortation to be faithful to the national God. One characteristic feature is the insistence on a single central sanctuary, at which alone sacrifice may be offered. The book concludes with a notice of Moses' death.

We now turn to the individual books. Genesis starts with the creation of the world, and carries the story down to the death of Joseph. It falls into four main sections :

(i)   Chs. i-xi. Early stories, leading up to Abram.

(ii) Chs. xii-xxv. The life of Abram (Abraham), ending with a brief summary of his descendants, and followed in ch. xxvi by a few events in the life of Isaac.

(iii) Chs. xxvii-xxxvi. The life of Jacob.

(iv) Chs. xxxvii–l. The life of Joseph, with an interlude in ch. xxxviii describing an event in the life of Judah.

As soon as we read the book through, we are at once conscious of striking differences as between various parts of it. There are, for example, fairly long lists of names, giving the genealogies of the outstanding figures in the story, and of others in whom Israel was interested. These usually take a stereotyped form, and often give the traditional ages reached by various people mentioned. But at times there are points in the narrative which make us ask questions as to the structure of the book itself. We have, for example, two accounts of the way in which the world was made. It is not always easy to reconcile details given in ch. ii with those given in ch. i. Which was made first, man or the animals? Ch. i appears to say: the animals; ch. ii: Man. How were the animals produced? Ch. i, 24, speaks of the earth bringing them out; in ch. ii, 19, God "models" them, apparently using the same method already employed in making man (ii, 7). But the differences go further than this. It is possible to feel this even through the English translation; in Hebrew it is even more striking. Ch. i is dignified, stately, scientific, and offers almost an evolutionary account of creation. There are three acts of "creation," i.e. the production of something for which no materials, or only some of the materials, already exist. These are (a) dead matter (v. 1), (b) animal life (v. 21), and (c) human personality (v. 27). The intervening stages in the construction of the universe are carried out automatically by the existing products at the command of God; incidentally, it should be noted that the East never thinks of the vegetable world as being alive in the same way as the animal. For the rest we might almost be listening to a lecture delivered by a learned professor to a highly sophisticated audience.

With ch. ii, 4, we find ourselves at once in a totally different atmosphere. The world is wholly barren, for there is no one to cultivate it. So God "models" a man in clay, and breathes life into him. Then He plants a garden which provides the man both with a home and with work. But the man is clearly not satisfied; there is something lacking in his life. So God makes animals in the same way as He has made the man, and brings them one by one to the man. As each comes before him, the man makes an exclamation, and that becomes the name of the animal. A great lumbering beast comes along, for example, and the man opens his eyes and mouth very wide and says " Shor "; ever afterwards " shor " is the Hebrew word for an ox. But none of the exclamations suggests that the man has found what he needed; the experiment has failed, and God tries another method. He throws the man into a deep anaesthetic slumber and takes out one of his ribs. He is careful to mend the man again, and then " builds up " the rib into a woman. When the man sees her he cries " This is it!", " this is the thing!"—or something like that; the Hebrew can hardly be translated literally, and adds the name-exclamation " Wo-man "; for this came " from man."

Apart from all differences in detail, we have in this case a lovely story for small children or other unscientific people. It is addressed to a totally different audience to that presupposed in ch. i. Each narrative has the same essential truth to convey : God and God alone is the Maker of the whole physical universe, including the human species. But in each case that truth is presented in a form suited to a particular type of listener; neither would be convinced by what is offered to the other. That is how the real message of God always comes to men; it must be in a form which they can appreciate, just as they are. And when we are considering the structure of the book, it looks as if the two narratives had once existed independently, and were placed side by side in the final construction of the whole.

Sometimes we meet with apparent discrepancies within the same passage. Some of us have always been puzzled by details in the account of the flood. How many animals of each kind did Noah take into the ark? In ch. vii, 2, God tells him to take seven each of all " clean " beasts and birds, i.e. of those kinds which may be sacrificed to God or eaten by men. He is also to take two each of every " unclean " species. In v. 5 Noah does exactly as God had told him to do. But in vv. 8-9 he takes only two of every kind, clean and unclean alike. Then, again, how was the flood produced? In v. 4 it is due simply to forty days' rain; in v. 11 the whole frame of the universe collapses; water pours down through the sky and up through the earth from the great waste of waters in which the world is set. There are also arithmetical problems presented by the duration of the flood; sometimes it seems to be much longer than at others.

In view of what we have noticed in chs. i-ii, we may suspect
the original existence of two independent narratives. They
have not been placed side by isde, as in the creation narrative,
but interwoven with one another. Even from the English
version it is possible to separate them, and this can be done
much more easily in Hebrew; every word falls naturally either
into one or the other.[1] When this has been done, there
appears a certain similarity between the two narratives
here and those of Chs. i-ii. We have the same dignified
form in one (the " two-animal " narrative), and the same
simple style of approach in the other (the " seven-clean-
animal " narrative).

There is another fact which is much less stressed today
than it was two centuries ago, when it was the chief point of
difference noted. This is the use of the divine names. In ch. i
and in the " two-animal " narrative of the flood, the word
used is simply " God." In the other, in each case, it is the
special name of the God of Israel. The Hebrew form was
probably Yahweh (we are sure of the consonants, and the
vowels are nearly certain); the English versions represent it by
the word LORD, in small capital letters. If it is immediately
preceded by the Hebrew word for " Lord," then the divine
name is printed as " GOD." Now, according to Exodus vi, 3,
God had revealed Himself to the Patriarchs under the name of
" El Shaddai," and Moses was the first person to hear of him
as " Yahweh." It seems, as if one group of the narratives
included in Genesis held to this view, and avoided the use of
" Yahweh," while the other disregarded it. The general character of the former group suggests a priestly tradition, and
passages of this group are commonly indicated by the letter
P, the letter J being used for the other.

These are not the only cases in Genesis where we find
reasons for suspecting that more than one narrative has been
used. Thus in ch. xii, 10-20 we are told how Abram lied to
Pharaoh about his wife. In ch. xx we have a similar story, but
Abimelech, king of Gerar in Philistia, takes the place of
Pharaoh. In the first story the divine name is Yahweh, in the
second it is simply the common Hebrew word for God—
Elohim. It seems likely that the two came from different

[1] These and other separated narratives can be seen in *The Book
of Genesis in Colloquial Speech,* published by the National Adult
School Union.

traditions, though both may have had the same event at the back of them.

We turn to another story, ch. xxxvii, which tells us how Joseph roused the jealousy of his brothers, and was eventually taken down to Egypt as a slave. Two grounds for his unpopularity are given. On the one hand he is his father's favourite, and is given a fine coat with long sleeves, which means that he is not to share in the hard work of the shepherds. The other ground is that he has dreams of greatness, in which his brothers and even his parents bow down to him. Of course there is no reason why the two should not have found a place in the same story. But there are other doublets. In v. 21 it is Reuben who saves Joseph's life; in v. 26 it is Judah. Again, the two features might have occurred in the same story. But there is a real discrepancy in the name of the tribe which took Joseph to Egypt. Both Ishmaelites and Midianites appear in the story. In v. 27 Joseph is sold to Ishmaelites, and according to xxxix, 1 it is they who take him to Egypt and sell him there. In xxxvii, 28, however, it is Midianites into whose hands Joseph falls, and in v. 36 it is definitely stated that it is they who sell Joseph to Potiphar. Curiously enough, when we try to separate two narratives here, we find that we get one complete dream-Reuben-Midianite story, and one complete coat-Judah-Ishmaelite story. The divine name, it is to be noted, does not occur in this chapter at all; the analysis is simple and obvious without it.

The two types of narrative at which we are looking now are by no means so clearly distinguished as the two stories of creation or of the flood. They are addressed to very similar audiences, and belong to the same general line of tradition. The differences between them are very slight; the most obvious in the passages we are considering is the fact that in one case dreams are prominent and in the other they are not. It is in a dream that God tells Abimelech what Abraham has done, and it is in a dream that Joseph has his great future revealed to him. We are not told how Pharaoh discovered that Abram had lied to him, except that great plagues fell on him and his house. The dream *motif* may be a link between the Abimelech story and the " Midianite " story of ch. xxxvii. In any case, we seem to have a third class of narrative from which the Book of Genesis was constructed. The general suggestion, then, is that in structure the Book of Genesis is a combination

of three main types of narrative, P, J, and a third for which
the letter E (for Elohim) is used. There may be other
elements; ch. xiv does not seem to fit in with any of the three;
there is nothing else like it in Genesis. A few scholars have
questioned the accuracy of the analysis, and one or two doubt
the separate existence of the E tradition, but the great body
of Old Testament scholars would agree in general as to the
structure of the book. The same groups of material appear
again in the next three books, and discussion of the date and
authorship may well be reserved till we have looked at the
whole Pentateuch.

Broadly speaking, the parts of Genesis in which " Priestly "
writing is commonly identified by scholars are as follows :

i, 1-ii, 4 : Creation.

v (except v. 29) : An antidiluvian genealogy.

vi-ix (Combined with a narrative from J) : Noah and the
    Flood.

x (Combined with a genealogy from J) : The descendants
    of Noah.

xi, 10-27 : A genealogy, Seth to Abram, followed by
    vv. 31*f*.

xvii : The Covenant of circumcision made between God
    and Abraham.

xxiii : Abraham's purchase of the cave of Macpelah.

xxv, 5-20 : Death of Abraham and early days of Isaac.

xxvii, 46-xxviii, 9 : Jacob's departure to Paddan Aram.

xxxiv (Combined with material from J) : The story of
    Dinah.

xxxv, 9-13, 22-29 : Jacob's return from Paddan Aram.

xxxvi : Sundry genealogies.

xlvi, 6-27 : Jacob and his family go down to Egypt.

There are many small notices, but these are the main
sections.

Roughly speaking, again, the following sections are usually
ascribed to E :

xx : Abraham deceives Abimelech by saying that Sarah is
    his sister.

xxi, 6-21 : Hagar and Ishmael in the wilderness.

xxii, 1-13 : Abraham is told to sacrifice Isaac.

xxxvii (Combined with a narrative from J) : Joseph sold
    into Egypt by his brothers.

xl-xliii, xlv, 1-xlvi, 5 : Joseph in Egypt.

B

It will thus be seen that there is little drawn from the E strain of tradition till we come to the story of Joseph, where it forms the main thread.

The remainder, comprising the greater part of the book is normally assigned to J.

As we read through the whole, we become conscious of a great motif running through the book. From the time when man was created in the image of God, and from his failure to maintain his position, there is a single purpose. A nation is to be chosen, which shall be God's in a special sense. Again and again it seems that this purpose will be frustrated, either by accident or by some evil in man. So terrible is this latter that at one point practically the whole race has to be destroyed; only eight persons are left alive to make a fresh start. The line is narrowed down to a single individual in Abraham, and for long years it seems that it will end with him. At last a legitimate heir is born to carry on the true succession, but even he has to run the risk of being sacrificed in accordance with a familiar ancient law that the eldest son must always be handed over to the deity. At the last minute he is saved, to beget two sons, of whom the chosen, Jacob, again has to pass through perils before his family is well established. At the last even he and his family are taken down to Egypt. Though all seems well when they first enter the country, it is not their real home; they are far from the land of promise, and are in danger of being absorbed in the ancient civilisation of the Nile delta. The reader awaits with anxiety and interest the next step. Can the chosen people recover their identity and their freedom? How will God deal with this new and even more serious situation? The immediate answer is given in the Book of Exodus, but in effect it occupies the whole of the Old Testament story.

CHAPTER III

THE LAW. 2

THE Book of Exodus recounts for us the events which made Israel a people with a particular national and religious life of their own. It takes up the story where Genesis left off, and gives a picture of Israel in Egypt some generations after the death of Joseph. Later tradition held that Israel was in Egypt for over four centuries; the genealogies in the Bible imply a very much shorter time. It may be assumed that these latter are reduced and summarised; on all accounts the period of residence must have been fairly long.

Briefly the outline of the narrative is this: The Egyptian king and his people have become alarmed by the growth of the Israelite nation, and are afraid of them. They reduce them to slavery, and try to keep down their numbers by destroying the male children. They fail in their attempt, though Hebrew mothers sometimes have to resort to desperate expedients. In one notable case, a mother hid her child for three months, and then exposed him in a covered basket by the river side. He was found by a royal princess, who was charmed by the baby, and adopted him. He became aware of his real parentage, and when he grew up took a practical interest in his own kinsmen. An act of violence in their defence compelled him to leave Egypt, and take refuge with a nomad tribe usually called Midianites, but sometimes Kenites. He married, and became a shepherd in his wife's family. One day, as he was tending his flock in a new area, he had an experience without parallel. He saw a deity in the form of fire, situated in a bush on a certain mountain. The deity revealed Himself as Yahweh, a God who had been accepted by the Patriarchs under the name of El Shaddai. Yahweh now ordered Moses to go to Egypt, lead the Hebrews out of the country to the sacred mountain where the revelation was taking place, and there hold a special "pilgrim-feast." Pharaoh and his people would be reluctant to let the Hebrews go, but Moses would be given special powers, and would bring plague after plague on Egypt till at last the natives would insist on their leaving.

Moses carried out his orders. As Yahweh had foretold, the Egyptian king refused again and again to release his slaves, even for a religious purpose. The appointed time for the festival, ever afterwards known as the Passover, arrived with the Hebrews still in Egypt, and, as they were unable to go to the spot sacred to Yahweh, Yahweh came to them, with disastrous consequences to the Egyptians. In the general confusion and terror Moses led his people out of the land. When the Egyptians recovered from their shock, they followed, and overtook the refugees by the "Sea of Reeds," traditionally identified with the Red Sea. Escape seemed impossible, but a way was miraculously made through the sea, and when the Egyptian forces followed the water came back and destroyed them. Thus the people were brought to realise that Yahweh was indeed a great God, and that He had delivered them.

They made their way to the sacred mountain, and there they entered into a covenant with Yahweh. As this is the most important event recorded in the Old Testament, it would be well to look at it more closely. To our minds, a " covenant " suggests something in the nature of a bargain, an agreement in which both sides undertake to observe certain conditions. But that is not what the term indicated to the Israelite mind. A covenant was essentially a unification of two or more parties which had previously been independent of one another. We may feel that there was a mystical element in the idea, but it was extremely powerful, and had most practical results. There might be conditions imposed by one side and accepted by the other, but these were not necessary, and served rather to define, and so to limit, the range of the Covenant. In the later history we hear of David and Jonathan making a covenant, but there is no suggestion of promises made by the one to the other; it is an act of blood-brotherhood. In Genesis xv Yahweh makes a covenant with Abraham, and gives him certain promises, but does not demand from the Patriarch any corresponding pledge of duty. And when the great Covenant is made at the sacred mountain, Israel has to accept terms and conditions, but none are expressly laid on Yahweh. What happens is that Israel and Yahweh are henceforward a vital unity; the formula He uses is, " I will become their God, and they shall become my people." Yahweh is now a member of the group, holding in it a unique position, but still one with His people.

The true nature of the Covenant appears when we look at the rituals by which it was established. Two of these are described in full. In Genesis xv Abraham takes a victim, kills it, cuts the body in two, and lays the parts on the ground, with a space between the head half and the tail half. Then he sees Yahweh, in the form of fire, passing through the little path between the two pieces. We may assume, from another reference to this same rite, that Abraham himself had already done this. The symbolism is clear. Each of the two parties has entered into the third, the slaughtered victim, and has come out of it. Its life, its vital essence, has been taken, and each of the parties is now identified with it; therefore each is now one with the other.

The second ritual form is that which is described in Exodus xxiv. Here we have on the one side an altar representing Yahweh, and on the other the elders of the people. These are the two parties who are to be united. Victims are killed, and their blood is drained off into bowls. Part is thrown over the altar. Then the elders hear the terms which are to be imposed on Israel; they accept them, and the rest of the blood is flung over them. The blood is, again, the vital essence of the victim; it now covers both parties, both are included in it, and therefore they are no longer two, but one in their identity with the victim.

We may compare such a simple action as the joining of two pieces of pipe to make a single long one. We take another piece of piping with an internal diameter equal to the external diameter of the pieces to be joined, and we fasten both into it. We now have one continuous pipe. So, in both these forms of covenant ritual there is a third party, whose life is given in order that the other two may be unified in it. We should do well to remember these facts in reading the New Testament, especially when we come to the words in which Jesus, at the Last Supper, stated the purpose of His own death.

The establishment of the Covenant is preceded in the narrative by a code of law; presumably its provisions are the conditions laid on the people for the making of the Covenant. It begins with the familiar " Ten Commandments," followed by a few regulations for the due performance of ritual; no metal figure is to be employed in Yahweh's presence, and special directions are given to ensure that the altar on which sacrifice is offered shall be built of earth and not of dressed stone. The main body of the code consists of what we should call civil and criminal law; the ancient world did not clearly distinguish between the two types.

Two features of this code may be emphasised. The first is that its provisions are adapted to, and indeed presuppose, the life of a settled community. There are provisions which would apply equally to nomad life, but there are others which have no meaning for a wandering group of shepherds. Oxen are frequently mentioned, and they have no place in the wilderness, where the animals may be sheep, but are more likely to be goats. They are certainly not large cattle. Laws which involve damage done by fire to field and vineyard (e.g. Ex. xxii, 5-6) have no meaning except in cultivated land.

The second point to be noted is that this code has remarkable parallels in other countries. We now possess copies of legal codes, in whole or in part, from Sumerians, Babylonians, Assyrians and Hittites. The oldest is that of the Sumerians, a people who preceded the Babylonians in southern Mesopotamia. Until quite recently this has been known only in fragments, but now a full text has come to light. It cannot be much later than the third millenium B.C. Next in order is the best known of all, that of Hammurabi, a Babylonian king supposed by many people to be identical with the Amraphel mentioned in Genesis xiv. This would make the code in the form it has come down to us contemporary with Abraham. In any case it is centuries older than the Exodus. The Hittite and Assyrian codes are still younger; both probably belong to the middle of the second millenium B.C.

Now while there are differences between all these, they have a common general pattern, and it is a striking fact that the same pattern appears in the code of Exodus xxi-xxiii. All five appear to be based on the same general principles, and cover much the same ground. All presuppose an agricultural and city-dwelling community, and considerable stress is laid on the rights of property. Slavery is a recognised institution, that temporary slavery with a limited term, which strikes us at once in reading Exodus. In Israel the period is six years, in Babylonia is was only three; in other directions the Biblical code is usually milder. One striking feature of the latter is that it suggests a much simpler order of society than any of the others. No class distinctions among free men are recognised; in Mesopotamia there was a clear difference between the gentry and the common people. In some instances we have laws in the code of Hammurabi which affect only special classes; medical men, for example, have special rules affecting their practice, intended to make them very careful in the way they treated their patients. But for the dates, we might have supposed that the " Book of the Covenant " was some centuries older than Hammurabi.

The remainder of the Book of Exodus contains both narrative and law. There is another code embedded in ch. xxxiv, which deals more with religious observances than with civil law. Chs. xxv-xxxi describe the steps by which Moses was to inaugurate the full religious life of Israel. These include plans for an elaborate tent which is to be the proper home of Yahweh. It looks as if a later generation had tried to picture Solomon's temple in a portable form, with wooden walls and curtains taking the place of stone, and we may guess that the tent actually put up by Moses was much smaller and simpler. We have also the ritual for the inauguration of the priesthood; Aaron, Moses' brother, is the first to be consecrated to this office.

Ch. xxxii tells the story of Israel's first great act of apostasy—if that is the right word to use of it. Moses was summoned to the top of the sacred mountain to receive further laws. He was away for nearly six weeks, and the people grew desperate. They had been led out of Egypt to find a God; they had lost their leader and had not found their God; at least they had not learnt the form under which He desired to be worshipped. So they came to Aaron for advice. He told them to give him what gold they had, and, according to the account he is said to have given afterwards, he melted it down and poured it out. Probably he poured it into water, believing that Yahweh would give it the form He prescribed as the metal suddenly cooled. Whether this was his idea or not, he found that the figure looked like a calf, and all the Israelites assumed that Yahweh wished to be represented by the image of a calf, or rather a bull. It is worth remembering that this view was held in Northern Israel at least from the death of Solomon to the destruction of Samaria. The rest of the story is familiar to us. It ended with Moses bringing down from the mountain two tablets on which he had written, at Yahweh's dictation, "ten commandments" (Ex. xxxiv, 28). The narrative does not suggest that these are our well-known "Decalogue," that stands at the head of the Book of the Covenant, and precedes the Covenant ceremony; these may be the ritual commandments contained in ch. xxxiv. In chs. xxv-xl the religious community is organised in accordance with the instructions previously given to Moses. And so the book ends with the community established as a nation, with a God who belongs to them alone, and to whom alone they belong.

Looking back over the Book of Exodus, we find that the same literary elements appear as those which we have seen in

Genesis. The priestly sections are easy to distinguish from their style, subject matter and general character. The main sections usually ascribed to this source are :

i, 1-5, 7, 13, 14 : Israel in Egypt.

vi, 2-vii, 22 : Moses receives his commission.

xii, 1-20, 43-51 (with a few verses between these sections) : Regulations for the Passover.

xiv, 1-4, 8-9 ,and occasional verse in the remainder of the chapter : The crossing of the Red Sea.

xvi, 1-3, 6-24, 31-36 : Incidents during the journey from Sinai, especially the giving of manna.

xxv, 1-xxxi, 18 : Instructions for making the sanctuary.

xxxiv, 29-xl : The building of the sanctuary and the in-auguration of the priesthood.

After iii, 15 the E tradition freely uses the divine name Yahweh, though Elohim often appears. It is thus less easy than in Genesis to separate E from J. This matters comparatively little, since both take the same general point of view, and were compiled in much the same period and at much the same stage of Israel's development. It is, however, usual to ascribe the " Book of the Covenant " to E and the " Ritual Deca-logue " in ch. xxxiv to J. Detailed analysis can be seen in any good modern commentary, though different scholars vary in minor points.

CHAPTER IV

THE LAW. 3

OF the next two books in the Law, Levticius contains an elaborate account of the Jewish ritual system, with special reference to sacrifice. Numbers is more varied in form and substance, and includes travel narratives, laws, and some ancient snatches of poetry.

Leviticus i-vii gives the prescriptions for sacrifice, i.e. animal sacrifice. In Israel, as elsewhere in the world, there were two main types of sacrifice. The one we may call a communion, the other a gift. In the former (simply " sacrifice " or " peace-offering ") the flesh of the victim is shared between God and the worshipper. When the victim has been killed, and the offal (including the skin) removed, a part is taken and burnt on a small altar. This is what the Hebrew word usually translated " burning incense " properly means. Part of the remainder is appropriated by the priest, and the rest cooked and eaten by the worshipper in the sacred precincts. Every temple was supplied with small rooms for this purpose. An account of the proceedings may be read in 1 Sam. ii, 12-17. This is an early type of ritual, and it gives the priests their share in the meal by what we should call chance; in the Law the portions were strictly defined.

The gift-sacrifice is usually called a " burnt-offering " or a " whole burnt-offering." It was handed over completely to God, and all except the offal was burnt on a large altar. There were special uses and some modifications in detail in types called the " sin-offering," the " trespass-offering," and the " guilt-offering." The most important of these was the " sin-offering," for only small parts were burnt as " incense," and the priests were allowed to eat those parts which were eaten by the worshipper in the communion sacrifice.

Chs. viii-x are especially concerned with the priesthood and its duties; in ch. x we have the story of Nadab and Abihu, who used the wrong spices. Chs. xi-xv deal with matters of ceremonial cleanness and uncleanness. These include dietary laws, the diagnosis of leprosy and the treatment of the leper, followed by rules of sex hygiene. Ch. xvi gives the prescription for the great annual Day of Atonement.

Naturally, these chapters are commonly assigned to the priestly element in the Law. The remainder of the book deals with similar subjects, occasionally adding details. There are, however, striking differences in style and general approach. We feel that the laws are aimed at keeping the people free from such impurity as might unfit them for the true worship of Yahweh, or even for membership of His community. One phrase is characteristic : " I am the Lord your God." It occurs some twenty-five times in the whole of the Law, and fourteen of these instances are in Lev. xvii-xxvi. Lev. xi, 44 is the only other place in Leviticus where it occurs. It is also characteristic of Ezekiel. In view of these facts, the section is commonly regarded as a separate division, and designated " The Law of Holiness." Ch. xxvii seems to be a kind of appendix to the whole book, dealing with the payment of vows.

With the Book of Numbers we resume the general history of Israel before the settlement in Palestine. First we have a census, taken at Sinai, followed by a system of organisation (chs. i-ii). Chs. iii and iv deal with the Levites in the same way, but in more detail. In chs. v and vi we have further laws dealing with special subjects, such as the ordeal of jealousy and the Nazirite vow; at the end comes the great blessing which stands apart both from what precedes and from what follows. The sanctuary is set up and the regular service is inaugurated (vii-viii). A year is thus occupied and the Passover is observed for the second time (ix, 1-14). The normal method of travel is described, with the guidance given by the pillar of cloud and fire which indicates the presence of Yahweh (ix, 15-x, 28). All this is written in the spirit and the style of the priestly element in the Law.

The general narrative is resumed in x, 29, and we are back once more in the world of J and E. Hobab, Moses' father-in-law (or is it brother-in-law?) leaves the people; in Ex. xviii, 1 and elsewhere he is called Jethro; perhaps there are two traditions or Moses had more than one wife. Quails and manna are sent, and the former produce a plague among the people. The narrative here, in Num. xi, is not unlike the earlier story in Ex. xvi; the two may come from different sources. Ch. xii tells us of an attempt made by Aaron and Miriam to challenge the authority of Moses. In xiii and xiv we have the story of the spies, and of the refusal of Israel to enter Palestine from the south. Here we seem to have a mixed narrative; some verses suggest the priestly type and others that of J and E. xv-xix, again are all priestly, except for a JE element which appears in xvi. These chapters are mainly concerned with the priestly office, and include the rebellion of Korah, Dathan, and Abiram. Aaron's position is established by the miracle of the sprouting rod (xvii). Ch. xviii prescribes the offerings on which the priests are to live, and xix gives instructions for preparing a sacred water of purification.

Ch. xx resumes the narrative of the wanderings. Once again Moses draws water from the rock (xx, 1-13), and the Edomites refuse to allow Israel a passage through their territory (xx, 14-21). Aaron dies at Mount Hor (xx, 22-29). There is war with southern Canaanites (xxi, 1-3), and in xxi, 4-9 the Israelites are punished for their murmuring against Yahweh. This is the familiar story of the "fiery serpents," which are not of any species known to zoologists, but special divine ministers; they appear under the name "seraph" in the great vision seen by Isaiah (Is. vi). Most of this is ascribed to JE, though there are verses, especially in ch. xxi, which suggest rather the priestly writing.

The remainder of ch. xxi is chiefly occupied with the story of Sihon's defeat. It includes several very ancient folk-songs, now difficult to understand. These appear to have been handed down from remote antiquity, and preserved in order to maintain Israel's claim to parts of the country between the Arnon and the Jabbok. This was always debatable land between eastern Israel and Moab. The territory of Sihon was, in fact, the first district in which any of the Hebrew tribes established a permanent home. The narrative is mainly JE, with some priestly admixture.

Chs. xxii-xxiv tell the story of Balaam, and of Balak's unsuccessful attempt to destroy Israel by magic. There were, however, more subtle dangers in contact with Moab, and ch. xxv tells the story of moral contagion which did immense harm to Israel while they were in that area. The general facts are derived from JE, but vv. 6-18 add details in which Phineas, the son of Eleazar, distinguished himself by his zeal, and so helped to confirm the position held by the house of Aaron. This, apparently, comes from a priestly source.

A similar origin has been ascribed to the rest of the book. Israel is now on the eastern border of Palestine proper, and will soon be attempting the conquest of western Palestine; the wanderings are nearly over. Ch. xxvi gives the figures of a new census, and in xxvii we have a narrative which defines the law of inheritance in cases where there are no male heirs. Chs. xxix and xxx contain more law, expanding and repeating much that has gone before. In ch. xxxi we hear that Midian is annihilated, and this gives occasion for a law prescribing the division of spoil after a successful campaign. Ch. xxxii records the settlement of the more pastoral tribes to the east of the Jordan. xxxiii-xxxv, 8 gives a summary of the stages and of the camping grounds used by Israel during the wanderings, and the rest of ch. xxxv limits the operation of the blood-feud by appointing "Cities of Refuge." The last chapter in the book is an appendix to the law of inheritance already given in ch. xxvii.

Deuteronomy stands entirely by itself. It introduces a new feature into Israelite literature, a fine rhetorical prose. The people are about to enter western Palestine. Moses is not to go with them, and he hands over the leadership to Joshua. But before leaving his people for that mysterious final resting-place which no man knows, he gives a last exhortation to the people, summing up the history of the wanderings and its lessons, and repeating a number of the laws which have been given. Then he goes away alone into a mountain from which he can see spread before him the whole breadth of the promised land, and lies down to die. God alone knows where he is buried.

The book opens with two addresses, sermons, or speeches, by Moses. The first, which occupies chs. i-iv, is a summary of the events which have taken place since the delivery of Israel from Egypt. Chs. v-xi form the second, an exhortation to obey the Law, with some indication of the disasters which will follow disobedience. It is not punishment, however, which is most prominent in the appeal. While Yahweh is presented as a God who insists on His rights and demands that He alone is to be worshipped by His people, the main stress is laid on His love for them and the love He asks from them. It is recognised that settlement in a land like Palestine, with a long established religion of mixed polytheism and animism, is full of dangers, and Moses does his best to strengthen and reinforce their mind and character. Nowhere else in the ancient world do we find so high an ideal of religion as that presented to us in Deuteronomy and other parts of the Old Testament comparable to it, and it is only in the New Testament that we find its true and perfect development.

Two passages call for special comment. It is interesting to note that the only part of the Exodus law to which Moses calls attention is the Decalogue. In Deut. v, 6-21 we have a form which differs very little from that of Exodus xx, 3-17. The most striking variation is to be seen in the law of the Sabbath. Instead of " Remember " Deuteronomy has " Keep," and it gives a different reason for the institution of the day of rest. In Exodus the reference is to the divine rest after creation (Gen. ii, 2f); in Deuteronomy the reason is humanitarian, resting on the need of man's servants and domestic animals. And in the tenth commandment a different word is used for "covet." But in essence the two sets of commandments are the same.

In Deut. vi, 4-9 we have a passage which is commonly known as the " Shema," from the Hebrew word for " listen " with which it begins. This is the heart of Moses' message, of the whole book, and, indeed, of the complete Old Testament. It was cited by Jesus as the first of all the commandments, and it still remains the supreme duty in both Judaism and Christianity : " Thou shalt love the Lord thy God with all thy heart and with all thy soul and with all thy strength."

After these two introductory discourses there follows in chs. xii-xxvi the legal code. It is in many ways closely parallel to the " Book of the Covenant " in Ex. xx, 22-xxxiii, 19. But it is clearly a revised form of that code. There are occasional modifications of laws, generally making them milder or more generous. Thus when a slave finishes his period of service, Ex. xxi, 3f enjoins that he shall go free exactly as he was when he became a slave. Deut. xv, 13-15 insists that he is to receive a gift from his master, which will enable him to start free life once more for himself. The reason given is significant; Israel has learnt by experience what it is like to be a slave, and must therefore treat slaves with compassion and liberality.

There are also numerous additions, many of which breathe the same spirit. Thus a bird sitting on eggs may not be taken, though the eggs may be removed. A parapet must be erected on the flat roof of every house, or someone may fall over by accident (Deut. xxii, 6-8). The treatment of a female captive prescribed in xxi, 10-14 is far more sympathetic than that which was usually accorded to women in such circumstances, and the protection afforded to an escaped slave (xxiii, 15f) is another example of the general tone which pervades this book.

The outstanding feature, however, of this code appears at the beginning, in ch. xii. Throughout most of the monarchical period it is clear that there were numerous sanctuaries to Yahweh in Israel. In many places altars might be found and used for sacrifice. Solomon received his divine communication at Gibeon, Samuel was in some way attached to the " High Place " at Ramah, and Elijah had no compunction about repairing and using an altar on Mount Carmel. Archaeologists, too, tell us that temples to Yahweh were found in other places than Jerusalem. Even as late as the fifth century B.C. a Jewish settlement in Egypt had its own temple, and could appeal to Palestine for help in restoring it after a Persian-Egyptian "pogrom." But in these two chapters of Deuteronomy it is expressly and emphatically laid down that there should be only one altar in the whole country. The location is not specified; the sanctuary at Shiloh was probably assumed to be the legal predecessor of that which was later built in Jerusalem. It was not till late in the seventh century that this regulation became effective in the life of Israel.

Ch. xxvii gives instructions for the acceptance of the Law when the tribes enter Palestine, and follows this with a list of curses to be pronounced on certain classes of offenders. In ch. xxviii we have a solemn warning of the consequences which will follow on the exact observance and on the neglect of the Law, and in xxix-xxxi we have the last address of Moses and the arrangements made for the leadership of the people after his death.

Chs. xxxii and xxxiii give us two poems. The first is the well-known Song of Moses, a great hymn of praise to Yahweh. The second is a series of short tribal songs, which should be compared with the parallel collection in Gen. xlix. There are striking differences between the two; the earlier passage seems to be composed of songs, or perhaps rather simple epigrams, on the separate tribes, while the " Blessing of Moses " looks like a single composition. The arrangement of the tribes is different; in Deuteronomy Simeon is not mentioned, while Levi is recognised as the priestly tribe, in strong contrast to the picture of a bloodthirsty people which is given to us in Genesis.

Finally, in ch. xxxiv, we have the account of Moses' last days, of his lonely climb to the summit of Pisgah, his view of the promised land, which he was not to enter, and of his quiet surrender of life to that God who had called and guided him to do a work unique in human history.

CHAPTER V

THE LAW. 4

TRADITION, accepted without question in New Testament times and for centuries later, ascribed the whole of the Law as a written document, to Moses. To many minds the authorship seems to be essential to faith in its divine inspiration, but a moment's reflection will show that the human instrument is of secondary importance to people for whom a divine origin is an effective article of faith. Doubts as to the accuracy of the tradition go back at least to the twelfth century, but it was not till the middle of the eighteenth century that they were taken seriously. It was only then that the study of the literary structure came to the front, and many scholars since that time have been convinced that the Pentateuch in its present form is the result of a growth spreading over many centuries. The position of Moses as the founder of Israel's nationality and religion has never been seriously questioned, and any who feel it essential to their faith in the inspiration of Scripture to maintain the actual authorship of Moses should, as one modern scholar has remarked, hold that position ' in all charity and give thanks to God.'[1]

There are three stages in the scientific study of any ancient body of literature. These are (a) its structure, (b) its date, or the dates of different elements in it, (c) the authorship of the parts or of the whole.

(a) It has been noted from time to time in the last three chapters that there appear to be four or five strands of literary material. Two of these, indicated by the letters J and E, are easily distinguishable in Genesis, but are less obviously separable in Exodus and Numbers, though it seems clear that both are present. A third strand is to be seen in Genesis, Exodus, Leviticus and Numbers, whose general character suggests an ecclesiastical origin. In Leviticus we have noted that one section, chs. xvii-xxvi, has a special atmosphere of its own, and while the greater part of this type of material is indicated by the letter P, these chapters are often separated and are mentioned by the symbol H (Law of " Holiness "). In the Pentateuch, Deuteronomy stands by itself, and we use the letter D when we speak of it, and of passages outside the Pentetauch which appear to be influenced closely by it.

In what order are we to place these strands? When we compare the two accounts of the Creation given in Genesis i and ii, we are at once struck by the extraordinary difference

[1] For the general position the student is recommended to consult *Pentateuchal Criticism* by D. C. Simpson (1924). Though some interesting suggestions have been made since this book was published, the broad outline of the subject is not seriously affected.

between them. This is largely obscured by the smooth and uniform translation into English which we find in the Authorised and Revised versions, but it is inescapable in Hebrew. It is not a mere question of style and vocabulary, but of the whole character of the two narratives. Ch. i is written in a stately and rather formal style. Its approach is philosophical and scientific, and its main outlines do not greatly conflict with the views of modern scientists. For example, the three acts of creation, matter, life and human personality, occur at points where theories of evolutionary process have not yet bridged a gap. But the second chapter reads like a nursery story. The earth is taken for granted, vegetation is first produced, and then man is " modelled " from clay, and given life by the breath of Yahweh. A similar process is used to make the animals, which are brought into being in an unsuccessful attempt to find a companion for the man. The desired end is achieved by a totally different method; the man is thrown into an anaesthetic slumber and a rib taken from him. Yahweh " builds " this into a woman, and the man's exclamation when he sees her shows that this experiment has succeeded.

One fact is obvious. Both these passages state that God is the creator of the universe, including mankind, but that eternal truth is presented in forms suited to widely different types of mind. The one is scientific, philosophical, sophisticated. With Gen. ii, 4, we pass into a world totally different from that in which we have read ch. i. It is, of course, possible that the two are contemporary, one being addressed to a highly " sophisticated " audience and the other to a far more elementary section of the community, but to many readers it will seem more probable that these two are separated by some centuries of growth and education. So we may well feel that J (and E goes closely with J) is earlier than P, though the latter may, and almost certainly does, include much early, even primitive, material.

It is usual to think of E as being addressed to an audience of rather higher development than that presupposed by J. There are slight differences; in particular the theology of E is less " anthropomorphic " than that of J. We can hardly imagine E telling the story of creation in the language of Gen. ii, and when God appears to men, he adopts a human form in J, but commonly speaks through dreams in E. These characteristics may help us to distinguish the two, but we are less safe when we assume that they come from different periods. Indeed, it is often held that the one is northern ("Ephraimite"), where a higher standard of culture seems to have been reached than in the south, where the "Judahite" traditions took shape. We are on surer ground when we regard J and E as being more or less contemporary.

Where does D come in? It is clearly later than E; indeed it is curious to find that in many ways it seems to be a revised and expanded form of E and to disregard J almost completely. In particular, the code of laws in Deut. xii-xxvi is at least based on Ex. xx-xxiii which is generally ascribed to the E tradition. One or two modern students have suggested that the differences here, as in the case of J and E, may be due to local and not temporal causes. But it does not seem likely that this view will be so fully adopted as to supersede the theory that D is later than J and E. There is also one provision in D of which E makes no mention. That is the law of the single altar and sanctuary, which is so emphatically stressed in Deut. xii. It looks as if D were here introducing a novelty, for several adjustments have to be made. It is assumed that there have been a number of altars at which a man in danger might take refuge (*cf.* Ex. xxi, 13*f.*). If there were only one altar in the land, people living at a distance from it would find the provision of little value. So six "cities of refuge" are appointed to take the place of the altar, and they appear again in the P section of Numbers. Further, the priests of the local sanctuaries have been living on the offerings of the people. These are no longer available, and they are told to come to Jerusalem and share with the existing priesthood the offerings made there (Deut. xviii. 6*ff.*). A third difficulty lay in the principle that the flesh of domestic animals might be eaten only in sacred precincts, as a "peace-offering." This would mean that distant communities could eat beef or mutton only by making the long journey to Jerusalem. So in Deut. xii, 20*ff* the flesh of the domestic animals is "secularised," and might be eaten at any time; the only restriction is that the blood must be poured out on the ground, for it is too holy for human consumption. We are fairly safe in placing D later than J and E.

But how is D related to P? We have already seen reasons for placing P later than J and E, but it does not follow at once that P is also later than D. Here, however, the character of the priesthood may help us. We have just seen that the priests of the old local sanctuaries were given permission by D to come up to Jerusalem and take their place beside the priests already there. But Ezekiel will have none of this. These local priests have ministered at improper shrines, many of them, no doubt, ancient Canaanite sanctuaries which have been converted to the worship of Yahweh—and retained some of the old vile practices (Ez. xliv, 9ff.). They are to be regarded as foreigners, and to be allowed only to perform menial duties about the sanctuary. The officiating priesthood is to be confined to the family of Zadok (Ez. xliv, 15ff.). Now in Deuteronomy all priests are regarded as equally sons of Levi, but in P, while all priests belong to the tribe of Levi, the term Levite is properly applied only to the subordinate ranks who do the menial work, while the priests proper are all descendants of Aaron. In this respect, then, Deuteronomy stands between the wide range of the priesthood in J and E and the narrowing down to a single family in P. Further, it is to be noted that we do not get from P that sense of disgust and almost hatred which Ezekiel seems to have felt for these inferior orders of clergy. The facts justify us in placing P after D, though it must be remembered, indeed insisted, that P may contain material which is very ancient; the ritual of the " scapegoat " on the Day of Atonement (Lev. xvi, 10, 21ff.) is a good example.

(b) The generally accepted order, then, is JE, D, P; H, when separated from the rest of P, may be placed about the same period as D or Ezekiel. But this does not settle the actual dating, and here there is more variety of opinion, though most scholars would still be agreed in the main. Clearly, if we can establish the approximate date of one of the strands, we can get nearer to the others also.

Now it has long been held that the book of the Law discovered in the Temple under Josiah (621 B.C.) is to be identified with Deuteronomy, or with an early form of that book. There are two reasons which may be mentioned. The first is that the reform of Josiah seems to be based on the law of the single altar. The historical records make it clear that this rule was unknown throughout the period of the monarchy.[1] Either, then, the book had been hidden at a very early period, or it had been composed fairly recently and " planted " not long before the repair of the Temple brought it to light. As against the first alternative, the law of the single altar

[1] *cf.* p. 29.

seems to have been unknown even to Samuel, a generation or
more before the Temple was built. In favour of the second
alternative, it may be noted that in the book of Jeremiah we
have a good deal of rhetorical prose which, in style and outlook, closely resembles the discourses at the beginning and end
of Deuteronomy. Ezekiel, too, has a style which is not so near
to Deuteronomy as that of Jeremiah, but is distinctly reminis-
cent of it. It should, however, be remarked that some scholars
would regard the sections mentioned in the Book of Jeremiah
as being a late and conscious imitation of Deuteronomy.

Further, it has been pointed out that the tone of
Deuteronomy, with its intense stress on the worship of
Yahweh as the only God for Israel, together with the strong
emphasis on the ethical and humanitarian tone of the laws, as
contrasted with those of Exodus, suggests the influence of the
great eighth-century prophets. It has, then, been widely held
that it sprang from followers of these prophets, and represents
their theory of the way in which their principles might be
carried into practice. It should, however, be remarked that
isolated scholars have differed here, some going back as far as
the time of Samuel, and others as far forward as Ezra. But
no two of these diverging scholars have agreed on the general
date.

The dating of the other elements is less certain. It is, however, widely held that P is connected with Ezra, and that the
law which he promulgated (Neh. viii) was either P or a part
of it. Time would not have allowed the reading and interpretation of the whole Pentateuch, and we gather from the
narrative that there was a certain novelty about the law introduced by the great Scribe. The date was either 458 or, more
probably, 398 B.C. In any case we may regard the adoption of
the Priestly writing in more or less its present form as being
post-exilic.

How far back are we to go with J and E? Here we have
practically no reliable data. There is, however, a general impression that they were compiled in the middle of the
monarchical period, since they appear to reflect conditions and
thought in the age of the great prophets.

(c) Only those who are able to ascribe the whole Pentateuch
to Moses can claim any exact author for the Law. Others must
rest content with a number of unnamed and perhaps insignificant people. For it would seem that many have taken part in

transmitting the words of these five books. We think of ancient narratives handed down from one generation as shepherds watched their flocks by their camp fires, of stories told to worshippers at the sanctuaries by the priests, of instruction given as to the right methods of worship in the same conditions, of local and tribal customs hardening into law, and harmonised as the sense of unity grew through the centuries, of scribes putting together what tradition had laid in their hands, and of the men who, especially in the Exile, maintained their faith and fitted it for transmission to those who should come after them. But however it came, it goes back to a divine Author, through whose working in the souls of men there was achieved a Law which made Israel the " People of the Book," and so played a major part in making ready for the coming of the Christ.

CHAPTER VI

THE FORMER PROPHETS : JOSHUA

THE Book of Joshua is the connecting link between the Pentateuch and the later historical books. The story of Israel's liberation from Egypt is incomplete until the people are firmly established in the promised land, while the narrative of the conquest is a necessary basis for the story of the nation, its rise, decline, and fall. It is, however, more closely bound to the Pentateuch than to the Book of Judges, both as history and literature. We still see the new nation acting and moving as a whole, under a single leader; we have not entered the phase of local and tribal isolation which preceded the foundation of the monarchy. Further, we observe the literary strands which have already been noted in the Pentateuch, and though some scholars have found J and E in succeeding books, the general opinion is that these documents, in so far as they were documents and not merely lines of tradition, do not extend into the Book of Judges.

The subject of Joshua is the conquest of western Palestine. The east has already been occupied, and henceforward Israel claimed Transjordan from the Damascus area to the Arnon. Moab, however, insisted that the true boundary was the Jabbok, and the territory between these rivers remained debatable land till the whole was absorbed in the Assyrian empire. The theory which is most obvious in the book is that the tribes first crossed the Jordan, then proceeded to conquer the land, acting as a single national and military unit. When the conquest was complete, and the original inhabitants exterminated, the country was formally divided as between the tribes. There are, however, traces of another tradition, which reappears in the opening chapter of Judges. This represents the tribes acting more or less independently. We have hints of this second interpretation of history in the account of the distribution of the land, especially in chs. xiv-xvi. Here Joshua gives the tribes of Judah and Joseph the duty of expelling or destroying the Canaanites from the portions of land assigned to them, and they are not wholly successful (cf. xv, 63, xvi, 10).

The book falls into two parts. Chs. i-xii describe the actual conquest, and xiii-xxiv the distribution of the land between the tribes. In the first part there are occasional verses which seem to have been inserted by an editor who wrote in the style and spirit of P, but the main narrative clearly recalls the J and E strands of the Pentateuch. Thus the exact figures and dates given in iv, 13 and 19 are quite characteristic of the Priestly school. There is, however a good deal of material which strongly suggests the style and outlook of D. Practically the whole of the first chapter belongs to this class, and there are short passages throughout chs. ii-xi which belong to the same general group. Occasionally these are rather longer, e.g. viii, 30-35 is clearly related to Deut. xxvii, 12-26. Ch. xii, too, is an example of that same desire to summarise history in order to draw a lesson from it which we find in the opening chapters of Deuteronomy. We get the general impression that the writer(s) of Deuteronomy, or some others who had accepted its points of view and studied its language, took the narratives of J and E, revising them and adding to them, in its spirit.

Ch. i describes the immediate preparations for the crossing of the Jordan, with special stress on the encouragement given to Joshua and the behaviour of the Transjordan tribes, who undertake their share in the actual conquest. Ch. ii records the experiences of the spies who are sent to look over Jericho, and the arrangement made by them with Rahab to secure her safety and that of her family. Then (chs. iii-iv) come the final instructions. The Ark is to lead the people as far as the middle of the river bed; there it is to halt, and wait till the whole army has gone over. Yahweh himself is to be the first to enter the river and the last to leave it. The instructions are carried out, and as soon as the Ark enters the river the stream runs dry. The reason is a stoppage much higher up, at Adam or Adamah, some twenty-five miles above Jericho, near the point at which the Jabbok enters the Jordan. Such stoppages are known to have occurred at other times, owing to great falls of rock and earth from the cliffs above the river. In the present instance the fall may have been due in part to an earthquake.

Special arrangements are made to ensure that the crossing of the Jordan shall never be forgotten. As our narrative stands, two great cairns are erected. One consists of stones taken from the river bed, and set up on the western side at the first place where the people encamped (iv, 1-3, 8). Also twelve stones are taken, apparently from the east side of the river, and set up in the middle of the stream, at the spot where the priests had stood with the Ark. It is assumed that the top of this cairn would be visible when the flow of water was resumed, and men would be told of its origin (iv, 4-7, 9). Possibly we have here two traditions which have been combined to form a single narrative. The people then proceed to make their first camp at Gilgal, in the Jericho plain, and this spot remains their headquarters until the conquest is complete.

The story of the conquest proper begins with ch. v. The first step is to circumcise the people. Circumcision appears to have been originally an African rite, practised among Semites only when the Egyptian influence was strong. Egypt had been the dominant power in the Palestine area since the middle of the fifteenth century, and the only uncircumcised group was that of the Philistines, whose invasions took place when Egyptian power was declining, at the end of the thirteenth century B.C. It had been practised during the residence in Egypt, but had been neglected since the escape of Israel; this seems to be implied in the phrase "the reproach of Egypt" (v. 9). At Gilgal Joshua receives a vision; a divine messenger, the captain of Yahweh's host, appears to him and indicates that the place is holy. From that time onwards Gilgal is recognised as one of Israel's sacred spots.

Ch. vi tells the familiar story of the way in which Jericho

fell. Modern excavation has shown that its walls collapsed owing to an earthquake, and fell outwards. Joshua pronounced a curse over the site, and no fresh city was erected on the ruins until the middle of the ninth century B.C.

Jericho is in the plains, and to the west of it rises a steep and rocky mountain mass about three thousand feet high. There are comparatively few passes leading up into the hill country, but it was necessary for the Israelites to secure a foothold among the mountains. The first attempt was made on Ai. Archaeology has thrown some doubt on the historical accuracy of the story, since it appears that some centuries separated the fall of Jericho from the destruction of Ai. It is possible that a later conquest has been thrown back into the age of Joshua, to whom tradition would naturally tend to ascribe the whole occupation of Palestine. The value of the narrative lies, however, in the light it throws on some of Israel's beliefs and practices. We have first the *taboo*, the ban placed on the use of consecrated soil. Jericho is the " firstfruits " of the conquest, and must be " devoted." All that is destructible must be destroyed, and materials too solid for burning must be kept out of human reach. But Achan takes part of the spoil, and therefore he becomes infected with this dangerous sanctity. He hides it in his tent, and so all its occupants are in the same case. He and his will contaminate every one who comes into contact with them.

Next we have the insistence on the need for consulting God for every operation. If Joshua had sought divine guidance, he would have discovered that there was something wrong in time to avoid the disastrous panic before Ai. Further, the will of Yahweh might be made known through the sacred lot. No human power could arrange or control the lot; therefore God decided it. And by a process of elimination through the lot, Achan was identified.

Finally we note the execution of Achan. This is not punishment for his sin; it is the only process by which Israel can be free from the taint of " sanctity " which he carries with him. The same rule applies to all his household; they, too, must be destroyed. They are all stoned and burned, stoned that the actual killer may not come into physical contact with the victim, and burnt in order to remove completely the *taboo* which clings to them. It is a piece of spiritual disinfection. Joshua's measures are effective, and at last Ai is taken. It is not the first city to be captured, and the spoil is available for all Israel. The narrative suggests that this victory so completely secures the occupation of the hill country, that Joshua is able to carry out the commands specified in Deut. xxvii, and solemnly invoke the curses and the blessings prescribed for the hills of Ebal and Gerizim.

Ch. ix records the incident of the Gibeonites, who secured their safety by a trick, pretending that they were ambassadors from a distant land, seeking alliance with Israel. The narrative is evidently ancient, and explains the lowly position of the Gibeonite natives, possibly in connection with the "high place" which was still recognised as a legitimate sanctuary in the days of Solomon.

In ch. x we have an account of further conquests in southern Palestine. Israel has now secured a firm footing in the central hills and can look in other directions. It is curious that there is no mention of the capture of Bethel, which forms an important triangle with Ai and Gibeon. Its conquest is recorded in Jud. i, 22-25, a passage which may have been taken from the original narrative from which the compiler of Joshua drew his information. The story includes an ancient snatch of song, taken from a collection which has long since disappeared. It was called "The Book of the Upright," though the Hebrew term (*yashar*) may be a contraction for "Israel." It speaks of a day on which the sun was still and the moon stopped, that a nation might take vengeance on its enemies.

The occasion to which this old couplet is applied (Josh. x, 12*b*-13*a*) was a battle between Israel and a coalition of Canaanite rulers. They included the kings of Jerusalem and Hebron; of the other three, Yarmuth is in the foothills to the west of Jerusalem, while Eglon and Lachtish are in the plain further south-west. This confederacy made an attack on Gibeon, and Joshua came to its rescue. The battle was fought near Beth-horon, which stands at the head of one of the main valleys leading down from the hills into the coastal plain, north-west of Jerusalem. The Israelite victory was complete; the kings fled for refuge to a cave. They had been compelled to flee to the north-west, and were thus driven away from their own cities. Joshua took them from the cave, submitted them to a ceremony of degredation, and killed them. The capture of their cities does not seem to have been recorded in the oldest form of the narrative; Jerusalem, at least, was first taken by David. The list of cities whose conquest is ascribed to Joshua in x, 28-43 probably comes from a Deuteronomic reviser.

Ch. xi tells of conquests in the far north. Since there is no detailed account of the occupation of the plain of Esdraelon, it may be assumed that the conquests were made from the east, and that some Israelites crossed the Jordan between the Sea of Galilee and Lake Huleh. We note that the principal adversary is a certain Jabin, king of Hazor. His name appears again in Jud. iv, 2. With this victory the conquests ascribed to Joshua are complete. The older narrative ends with v. 9; vv. 10-15 seem to be from the hand of a Deuteronomic reviser. It will be remembered that in the theory of this school, the Canaanites ought to have been exterminated and that Joshua did his duty. The remainder of ch. xi and the whole of ch. xii are occupied with Deuteronomic summaries of the kings Joshua had overthrown and the peoples he had destroyed. In the light of later history it is impossible not to feel that this is an idealised picture of the past.

With ch. xiii the second part of the book begins. From the literary point of view, its structure has one striking difference from that of chs. i-xii. The earlier half of the book gives the impression of having been modified by a writer or writers of the Deuteronomic school. In chs. xii-xxii that element hardly exists, and while there are occasional verses which some scholars would ascribe to J and E, by far the greater part seems to be the work of priestly writers. We have an account of the ideal division of the land in the later chapters of Ezekiel, but it is hardly an actual sketch; the priestly writer, who has clearly some record of the facts at his disposal, is much more realistic, and has probably given us a fairly true picture of the land as it was during the period of the monarchy. It will be noted, for example, that the lot of Simeon is said to be within Judah (xix, 1), suggesting that this tribe ceased to maintain an independent existence early in the history of Israel.

The conquest being complete, the Transjordan tribes are dismissed with Joshua's blessing; before crossing the Jordan they erect a great altar to Yahweh. The suspicions of the western tribes are aroused, and they ask for an explanation. The reply is that this altar is not intended to rival the central sanctuary, but to serve as a reminder of the duty these pastoral tribes owe to their fellows on the west of the river, and with this Joshua and his people are content.

The final chapters of Joshua give an account of the hero's last words and death. Ch. xxiii, which is Deuteronomic in character, is an exhortation to the assembled people. They are reminded of the way in which Yahweh has fulfilled all his promises, and warned that their future success depends on their maintenance of the principles laid down in the Deuteronomic law. It seems that the conquest is not quite so complete as we had been led to suppose by earlier passages, for the greatest of dangers is that of mixing with the surviving Canaanites. Intermarriage is most strictly forbidden.

In ch. xxiv we have another address from Joshua, which seems to be taken from the older narrative, probably from E. It begins with a historical restrospect going back to the patriarchal age, urges the people to refuse all gods other than Yahweh, and states the determination of Joshua and his family to remain faithful to the national God. He recognises that originally the ancestors of the people had worshipped other gods, and that the nations about them still did so, but neither heredity nor environment is to affect them. The people accept the choice Joshua offers them, and agree to put away foreign gods which are still among them. The Covenant is renewed, and a great stone of witness is set up at Shechem. Joshua dies and is buried, the bones of Joseph, which Israel has carried through all their wanderings and their battles, are laid to rest, and finally Eleazar, who had succeeded his father Aaron in the priesthood, also dies and is buried. The old age has passed away; from patriarchal days Israel has been a nation of wandering shepherds. Now a new era is to begin, and we are to enter on the history of the people as they work out their destiny in the promised land.

CHAPTER VII

THE FORMER PROPHETS: JUDGES

IT is the Book of Judges which gives us a picture of Israel's early settled life in Palestine. In one sense it may be regarded as the completion of the conquest, in another it is the preparation for the monarchy. It presents to us a people divided by tribal and geographical distinctions, for the most part mixed a good deal with their predecessors, yet retaining a traditional unity in politics and, still more, in religion. There are periods in which the sense of unity is obscured, and seems almost to be in abeyance, but it always re-emerges and each fresh manifestation adds something to its content. There is no true centralised power; the common life of the community is best expressed in its religion, and even here, though the sanctuary which contains the Ark has a real pre-eminence, local shrines and altars are recognised.

As it stands, the book is in the main a collection of narratives which describe the exploits of certain heroes who had led their people to victory. All seem to have been local figures, whose work was done in a limited area, though they made their appeal for support to the whole of the ideal nation. The traditions have been collected and placed in order by a writer, or a school of writers, whose language and point of view strongly remind us of Deuteronomy. Here is a definite philosophy of history; Israel sins by forgetting Yahweh and adopting the local Canaanite cults. Punishment comes in the form of a foreign invader, who " enslaves " Israel for a number of years. Suffering leads to repentance, and Yahweh raises up a deliverer, a " judge " (the word has a much wider content in Hebrew than in English), who summons Israel in the name of Yahweh, and in His might overthrows the enemy and liberates his people. As long as he lives, the nation is faithful to its God, but on his death a new relapse begins, and the process is repeated. The theory is stated simply and clearly in ch. ii, and we note the tendency to regard the Judges as consecutive rulers of the whole land.

Ch. i forms an introduction, completing the narrative of the conquest, and laying a certain stress on the length of time it took and on its imperfect success. Much of what we read here can be found also in the later chapters of the Book of Joshua. At the end of the book we have the record of two events which may have taken place at any time during the period, and do not in any way illustrate the main theory of the book. One records the migration of Danites from their original home on the south-western seaboard to the far north (xvii-xviii). The other gives an account of an inter-tribal war in which Benjamin was almost exterminated (xix-xxi).

In all, twelve " Judges " are mentioned. Six of these, however, are minor characters, of whom there is only a passing notice, with reference to a single feat or peculiar feature. The deeds of the others are recorded at some length, and in one or two cases it seems that the narrative is composite. It is even possible that in one instance accounts of two different persons have been interwoven with one another. The six " major " Judges are :

1. Othniel (iii, 7-11). The oppressive enemy is Cushan-rishathaim, king of " Mesopotamia," who enslaved Israel for eight years. Othniel is related to Caleb, being either his younger brother or his nephew; the latter is the more probable meaning of a somewhat ambiguous Hebrew phrase. In Jud. i, 12-15 he is described as the conqueror of Kiriath-sepher, a place later known as Debir.

We have no clue to the identity of Cushan-rishathaim, but his name, which seems to mean " doubly-wicked black man," may well be a corruption of some foreign word, and the mention of Mesopotamia may carry this event back to a raid from the east on which we have no further information.

2. Ehud (iii, 12-30). Here we have far more detail. The oppressor is Eglon, king of Moab, whose domination lasted eighteen years. Deliverance comes when Ehud assassinates Eglon, and summons central Israel to drive out the Moabites. Obviously it is only western Palestine that is affected; the permanent conflict between Moab and the eastern tribes does not come into question. Even so late as the ninth century, when Mesha records his Israelite conquests, there is no mention of any place to the west of the Jordan.

3. Deborah and Barak (iv, 1-v. 31). This narrative belongs properly to the conquest, and describes how tribes in and about the plain of Esdraelon secured their independence, at least for a time. Two accounts have come down to us, one in prose and the other in poetry. They differ in one or two details. In ch. iv the " oppressor " is Jabin, king of Hazor, whom some would identify with the Canaanite king mentioned in Joshua xi, 1-9. His commander-in-chief is Sisera, and it is with him that the narrative is concerned. He alone appears in the poem of ch. v, and his death is the climax of the whole story. There seems to be also a discrepancy in the manner of Sisera's death. In the prose narrative, Jael kills him as he lies asleep under a rug; according to the poet she strikes

him down as his head is bent to drink from the milk she has brought him.

It is, however, clear that though we have slightly divergent forms of the story, the general tradition is common to both accounts. The poem is particularly important. It is, by general agreement, the work of a contemporary poet, probably an eye-witness of the events, or some of them, and is our best evidence of the condition of Israel in the earlier part of Israelite occupation. Several features point to a date earlier than the Philistine invasion and settlement. The poet seems to assume that the plain of Esdraelon is in Israelite occupation, and we know that by the time of Saul (eleventh century B.C.) it was held by the Philistines, whose garrisons reached as far as the ford of the Jordan at Bethshan. It was, indeed, from that area that the final attack on Saul was launched. But, further, the reference to Dan is most significant. In mon-archical times the tribe was located in the far north; " Dan to Beersheba " was the comprehensive expression for the whole length of Israelite territory. But there was a tradition which told of its establishment in the south-west of Judah. It is hardly conceivable that this position could be held after the Philistine invasion, for it was in that general area that their " pentapolis " was established. In Samson's day the tribe was limited to a small inland district containing two larger villages, Zorah and Eshtaol, and a hamlet known as " Dan-camp." And in Jud. xvii-xviii we have the account of a migration which set up the headquarters of the tribe at Laish.

Now in Jud. v, 17, Dan is among the tribes condemned for not coming to the help of Yahweh against Sisera, and it is described as " sojourning in ships," a phrase which, if it means anything at all, implies a residence on the coast. The Philistine migration was carried out by land and sea, and it seems impossible that the Danites on the coast should still remain an independent tribe capable of sharing in a military expedition. The Philistines were checked on the borders of Egypt in 1192 B.C., and it seems that we must place the " Song of Deborah " not later than the end of the thirteenth century B.C.

" Song of Deborah " is the name we commonly give to this poem, but it is unlikely, though not impossible, that the prophetess herself was the composer. In v, 1 Barak is asso-ciated with her, and that would explain the antiphonal address to Deborah and Barak in v, 12. But it seems far more probable that the exhortation to Barak is a part of the song, or spell, which Deborah is asked to pronounce. In v, 7 an ambiguous Hebrew form may be rendered " thou didst arise " rather than " I arose." But the actual authorship is of small importance compared with the fact that here we have a great literary monument from a period in which Israel was just emerging into the culture of the settled community. It still has the abandon of the wilderness, but, in spite of serious textual corruption, the form is fairly regular, and characteristic of Hebrew poetry.

There are several outstanding features in this picture of early Israel. There is practical disunion, each tribe maintaining its own independence. There is ideal union; all the tribes are parts of a single whole, and the unifying factor is their common worship of Yahweh. The tribes to the east of Jordan are condemned for their refusal to take a share in the enterprise; so, too, are the coastal tribes of Asher and Dan. An obscure place named Meroz (v, 23) is cursed for not coming to the help of Yahweh—Yahweh, not Israel. There is the fierce passion against an enemy, and the exultation over his fall; the vindictive fury of the poet is concentrated on an individual, and the climax of the whole is reached with his death. We could ill have spared this vivid picture of the distant past.

4. Gideon (Jerubbaal) (vi-viii). It is possible, as has been already suggested, that we have in this narrative a combination of traditions concerning two of the great heroes. There are interesting doublets; the hero has two names and two enemies, while the chiefs of these enemies bear different names, and suffer different fates. If there were originally two different narratives, they have been well combined, and their raids have been telescoped into a single invasion. The story of Gideon's call through a theophany is told more fully than that of any other " Judge," and he is clearly inspired by that power which came down on men from time to time. This is true of all the Judges, though it is not so strongly stressed in some other cases.

The two enemies are Midianites and a mixed group of Bedouin; Amalek is the only tribe mentioned by name, and the others are simply grouped together as " Sons of the East." The invaders are defeated by the familiar stratagem of the torches and the trumpets. While the others are mentioned, it would seem that here the Midianites were at least the most important group, even if they were not originally the only foes in this story. Gideon belongs to the tribe of Manasseh, but he sends to the Ephraimites, and urges them to seize the fords of the Jordan. They do so, and among their victims kill the Midianite chieftains, Oreb and Zeeb (" Raven " and " Wolf ").

Ch. viii tells us that Gideon pursued the two kings of Midian, Zebah and Zalmunnah, across the Jordan. He and his men asked the town of Succoth for supplies, which were refused; to the east of the Jordan the desert tribes were more dangerous than Gideon and his men. But Gideon overtook the two kings, and put them to death with his own hand. Great spoil was taken, and from it Gideon made certain sacred objects, which the compiler, writing in the spirit of Deuteronomy, strongly condemned.

The sequel to Gideon's story is an unsuccessful attempt to carve out a kingdom, made by his son, Abimelech. The narrative is contained in Jud. ix, and is an unpleasant story of cruelty and treachery. Abimelech's activities were confined to the Shechem district, and at his death no further attempt at a monarchy was made until the time of Saul.

5. Jephthah (Jud. x, 6-xii, 7). Jephthah is the one hero of the eastern tribes. Exposed as it was to the wilderness and the desert, his country was more liable to Bedouin raids than was western Palestine. The adversaries mentioned are Ammonites; they were the most easterly of the Palestinian groups, and were nearer to the nomads than their neighbours. It is, however, interesting to notice that when Jephthah comes to talk to the enemy about their respective frontiers, his arguments are addressed to Moab, not to Ammon (Jud. xi, 12-28). Have we here indication of a double tradition? Did one story tell of war against Ammon and the other of war against Moab?

The story of Jephthah is remarkable for two features. One is the appearance of human sacrifice. There is abundant evidence to show that the practice existed among most Semitic peoples down to a comparatively late period. Even in Israel it died hard, and Ezekiel assumes that the injunction to give the first-born to Yahweh was intended to enjoin the actual sacrifice of the child (Ez. xx, 25f.). The story told in Gen.

xxii shows that the true Israelite spirit revolted against it at an early period, but it was still practised occasionally at times of great stress or danger. It is clear that Jephthah expected a human victim, though he certainly did not wish his own daughter to be sacrificed. The narrative looks like one of those stories which are commonly told to explain an ancient practice. The wailing of the women probably goes back to a much earlier period than that of Jephthah, or even that of Israel's entry into Palestine. Be that as it may, Jephthah's daughter still ranks in our thoughts with Iphigenia, the virgin-martyr of Greek tradition.

The other incident is less striking, but has introduced a common phrase into our language. The Ephraimites were jealous of Jephthah's success, and their feeling led to armed conflict, presumably to the east of Jordan. They were defeated, but on their flight were intercepted at the fords over the river. The Gileadite guards applied a dialect test to every person who tried to cross. If they could pronounce the word " Shibboleth " in the normal way, they were allowed to go free, but the Ephraimite dialect could say only " Sibboleth," and those who failed in the test were put to death.

6. Samson (xiii, 1-xvi, 31). Samson is unique among the " Judges," and seems hardly to belong to that class. He is a local Danite hero, living during the first stage of Philistine aggression. He was a character remembered for his individual exploits, but he led no armies, won no victories, and exercised no governing power; he ranks with Hereward the Wake rather than with Joan of Arc. Yet he receives far more space than any other character in this book, and later generations have seized on his story as a fitting theme for tragedy. His exploits, depending on a God-given strength, have caught the imagination of all ages; his fall through the treachery of a woman, and the final scene in which he slew at his death more Philistines than he had slain during his lifetime, have a high dramatic quality which have been used again and again as the basis for performance in the theatre.

The structure of the Samson section is quite simple. It begins with an account of his birth, and of his pre-natal consecration as a Nazirite. The remainder is simply a collection of traditions recording his deeds and his hostility to the Philistines, deeds which are actuated by personal vindictive-ness rather than by patriotism or religion.

These, then, are the " major " Judges. Six others are mentioned : Shamgar (iii, 31), Tolah (x, 1-2), Jair (x, 3-5), Ibzan (xii, 8-10), Elon (xii, 11-12), and Abdon (xii, 13-15). None receives more than three verses; only Shamgar is said to have fought an enemy. The same name occurs in Jud. v, 6, but if the notice in iii, 31 has any historical value, they can hardly be the same person. The only facts recorded about the others are purely personal matters, such as the number of their children or details of their property and behaviour. They play no part in the history of Israel, and the only question they raise is that of their presence at all in the record. It may be that the compilers of the book wished in one way or another to list twelve " Judges," since that is the ideal figure for Israel.

As we have already noticed, the last two sections of the book stand outside its general plan. The first, chs. xvii-xviii, may be regarded as the sequel to Samson's story. He had not delivered even his own tribe from the Philistines, and they were compelled to migrate to the far north. There they established a sanctuary, and this story looks as if it were that which would have been told by the priests there, in explaining how and why the cult originated. In particular they would be anxious to show that the priesthood went back to Moses; indeed, in xviii, 30, the first priest is named Jonathan and described as the grandson of Moses.[1]

The last three chapters of the book describe a civil war in which the tribe of Benjamin was nearly exterminated. It began with a brutal outrage on the concubine of a Levite belonging to the tribe of Ephraim, perpetrated by the men of Gibeah. The whole people rose and demanded the punishment of the guilty. It was refused, and a holy war was proclaimed, one of the conditions being that no tribe should give its daughters in marriage to the Benjamites. After two serious defeats, the united nation was successful. Every Benjamite city was sacked, and all its inhabitants destroyed. Six hundred men alone escaped. In four months' time the people realised that one of the tribes was in danger of extinction, and determined to find wives for these six hundred

[1] As the text stands, it makes him the grandson of a certain Manasseh, but the word is written in such a way as to make it clear that the original form was Moses. To later scribes it was intolerable that any descendant of Moses should have been the priest of a shrine which was held to be illegitimate.

D

survivors. Jabesh Gilead alone of Israelite cities had taken no part in the war, and so had incurred the extreme penalty. The city was destroyed, and four hundred virgins saved, to become wives of Benjamites. Two hundred were still left unmarried, and advantage was taken of a festival at which the women went and danced in the vineyards. The two hundred lay concealed till the dance was at its height, and then rushed out from their ambush and carried off their wives. So the tribe was kept alive, though it never again reached its old size. Here, too, we probably have a narrative which was intended to explain some element in the common marriage ceremonial.

CHAPTER VIII

THE FORMER PROPHETS: I AND II SAMUEL

THE book of Judges ends with the words : " There was no king in Israel; every man did that which was right in his own eyes." The phrase had occurred before, and may be taken as the characteristic summing up of Israel's condition for some generations after the initial conquest. The next section of the Former Prophets is concerned with the establishment of the monarchy. It was originally a single narrative, but for convenience was divided into two parts, the death of Saul making a suitable line of demarcation. Here we shall consider it as a continuous document.

The Book of Samuel, then, falls into three parts : (a) Samuel (I Sam. i-xii), (b) Saul (I Sam. xiii-xxxi), (c) David (II Sam.). The consecutive sections overlap; I Sam. ix-xi describe the way in which Saul became king and his first great military exploit, though the formal introduction to his reign occurs in xiii, 1. There is a great deal of information as to David's earlier life in the Saul section, but the death of the first king forms an obvious break in the history.

The compiler of the book has used a number of sources. For the first two sections he has probably relied on traditions which were written down some time after the events which they describe. Stories may have been preserved at sanctuaries, such as that of Ramah and Jerusalem, where men told of the

Ark and its fortunes. Any records kept at Shiloh probably perished with the destruction of that city, but men would remember what they had been told. A similar fate befell Nob, but one of the priests escaped, to carry on the traditions of David's early life. It would seem that stories about the prophets were popular, and were from time to time put together in writing. Such collections, as far as we can judge, were made down to the period of the exile. We have no personal records of any post-exilic prophet, and our knowledge even of events in the life of Ezekiel is based wholly on what the prophet himself has reported. Towards the end of David's reign we may have extracts from the Temple narratives of Jerusalem, recording the way in which the sacred site was recognised and adopted. Finally, in II Sam, ix-xx we have what most scholars today regard as an extract from the contemporary annals of David's court.

The narrative opens with an account of the birth and early years of Samuel (i, 1-iii, 21). We have a detailed picture of family life in early Israel, and especially of the procedure at a sanctuary, presumably at Shiloh. After a family sacrifice and sacred meal, Hannah, wife of Elkanah, prays for a son and vows that if one is given to her he shall be dedicated to God. Her wish is fulfilled, and she sings a song of thanksgiving and triumph. The boy is brought to the sanctuary when he is old enough, and becomes one of the attendants. In the meantime, the sons of Eli, the chief priest of the shrine, have shown themselves unfit for their office, by refusing to accept that portion of the sacrificial meal which God saw fit to assign to them. They commit also other offences, and God appears to Samuel and warns Eli, through the boy, that his house is doomed. Samuel grows up, and is recognised as a " prophet "; this (iii. 20) is the only place in this book where Samuel receives that title.

In iv, 1-vii, 1 we have an account of a great Philistine victory, which resulted in the capture of the Ark. It is probable that Shiloh was destroyed at the same time; certainly the priestly house of Eli was extinguished. But though the Ark had been taken prisoner, Yahweh had not been defeated, and showed his supremacy by various acts of power. The Philistine god, Dagon, was compelled to worship Him, and plague, probably bubonic plague, broke out wherever the Ark was taken. Finally, in order to get rid of Yahweh the Ark was solemnly released, and guided the oxen by which it was drawn, to the Israelite city of Kirjath-Jearim.

Chs. vii, 2-viii, 22 form an introduction to the foundation of the monarchy. The section is opened with a passage which strongly recalls the Deuteronomic tone and theology. Owing to bad government by Samuel's sons, the people demand a king. Samuel protests, but Yahweh tells him that the real offence of the nation is religious and not political. Yahweh is the only legitimate king, but since Israel forsakes Him and asks for a human monarch, the people shall have their way. Samuel, however, is to warn them how the king will behave. The stage is now set for the entry of Saul.

Chs. ix-xii give us two accounts of the way in which Saul became king. In ix, 1-x, 16 we have the familiar story of his being sent to look for his father's asses, of his meeting with Samuel, and of the strange experience which followed. It is interesting to note the difference between the two men. Samuel is called a " seer," and receives his revelations in a quiet fashion. Saul, on the other hand, becomes a " prophet," joining with a band of wild ecstatics whom he meets coming down from the " high place," which is the local sanctuary, with music and dancing. This peculiar behaviour, due to some psychological abnormality, is ascribed to the onrush of the " spirit," a divine power which turns Saul into " another man." Throughout his life he was subject to attacks of this kind, and as long as he was happy in his sense of association with Yahweh, all went well with him. When that relationship was broken, he lost confidence, and the presence of the " spirit " became his bane. But for the time, he was strong in the feeling that he was doing the work of Yahweh in fighting the enemies of Israel.

The rest of ch. x gives us another picture. It follows directly on viii, 22 and develops the same theory : the monarchy is in a sense a piece of apostasy, since it means reliance on a human leader instead of on the divine Lord. But since Israel will not be satisfied without a king, they shall have one—and take the consequences. It falls to Samuel to see that their wishes are carried out, and he selects Saul by casting lots. This is one of the recognised methods by which the divine will might be ascertained. Every event is thought to be the result of a personal act of will. If it is completely beyond human power to arrange and control the event, that must be ordained by God Himself. No mere man can forecast or decide the issue of the lot, therefore it is an act of divine interference.

With ch. xi we are back again in the other and older narrative. Saul, in common with the rest of Israel, hears of an attack on Jabesh Gilead by the Ammonites. The prophetic spirit sweeps him away, and he sends a fiery message all through Israel, with the result that the people rally quickly to him, and with the forces thus secured, he saves the threatened city. Here he is acting as the old Judges had done, but the pressure of the Philistines makes it necessary that his power should be more highly organised and more durable. In other words, he must be a real king.

Ch. xii is Samuel's farewell to the people. He has now handed over authority to the king whom the people have insisted on having, and takes the opportunity of summing up his own work and making a final appeal to the nation. He attests his position by the miracle of a thunder storm at harvest time, i.e. in March or April, when rain never fell in Palestine. The chapter naturally falls into line with the later narrative, and its strongly Deuteronomic tone gives us a clue to the school in which it originated, or by which it was adopted.

(b) It is with ch. xiii that the compiler of the book opens his history of the reign of Saul. For the first time we have that formula which we meet in the historical books at the head of every king's reign, a note giving his age at his accession and the number of years he was on the throne. Unfortunately the figures do not seem to have been known to the writer, and the actual text runs : " Saul was a year old when he became king, and he reigned over Israel for two years." It is now generally held that the figures were simply left out. The text used by Greek-speaking Jews (based on the text as it was read in Egypt) either left out the verse altogether or made Saul thirty years old at his accession, while the tradition followed by St. Paul in Acts xiii, 21 gave him a reign of forty years. Both these statements look like attempts to fill up a gap.

The earlier part of the narrative which gives us the reign of Saul is occupied with his wars against the Philistines. Quite soon there is a breach between the king and Samuel; the latter insists that he alone can offer sacrifices, while Saul maintains his right to do so in emergency. Israel reaches a low and almost

desperate position, when an exploit by Jonathan changes the
whole situation. Together with his squire, the young prince
attacked a Philistine outpost on the central ridge, looking
down on the Jordan valley. Jonathan, in berserk rage, dashed
his enemies to the ground, and the squire followed him and
gave the *coup de grace* as the men lay on the ground. Panic
seized the Philistine garrisons, and the hill country was cleared
for the time. The rest of Saul's wars were fought on the lower
slopes, as he resisted the attempts of the Philistines to recover
their position in the central range.

All his life Saul had to contend with Philistine aggression.
For years his resistance was successful; the attacks were made
from the coastal plain, and the passes into the hills were
unsuitable for chariot manoeuvres. But at last they made their
base at Bethshan, and moved into the hills from the north.
Saul was defeated in the final battle on Mount Gilboa, which
looks down on the plain of Esdraelon, and committed suicide.
That, in short, is the historical substance of the narrative
contained in I Sam. xiii-xxxi.

There are, however, other matters in these chapters. Most
prominent among them is the gradual rise of David, and the
internal conflict may well have had a bearing on the issue of
the war. This element in the narrative begins with an expedition against Amalek. Saul is ordered by Yahweh, through
Samuel, to exterminate this tribe, and fails to carry out his full
instructions, for he saves alive Agag, the king of Amalek,
and keeps some part of the cattle which are captured. As these
had all been " consecrated," put under the sacred ban, Saul
and his people had committed an offence comparable to that
of Achan (ch. xv). Samuel is told to pronounce sentence on
Saul, and to anoint a son of Jesse in Bethlehem. He goes to
Bethlehem, and anoints David (ch. xvi, 1-13).

Next we have the steps by which David came into prominence. Here we have two narratives which it is difficult to
reconcile with one another. The first appears in ch. xvi, 14-23.
The spirit which has roused Saul to his triumphs now turns
against him, and his officers try to find some relief for the
king. One mentions, quite casually, that David is a good
harpist; we have already seen that music played a part in the
life of the " prophet." David is brought to Saul, and is
successful. A friendship springs up between the Bethlehem
shepherd and Saul, who makes the lad his squire.

In ch. xvii we have a very different story. David is still at home, but his brothers are in Saul's army. The lad is sent to them with a message and small gifts, and reaches the camp at a time when they are being defied by a Gittite giant. David overcomes and kills him, and is then taken into Saul's army. But the king has no idea who the young hero is until he is told (*cf.* vv. 31*ff.*, 55), and it is hardly conceivable that he had been for some time acting as the king's squire. It seems clear that we have here two totally independent accounts of David's introduction to Saul, which have simply been placed side by side. It may be added that in the second account it is Saul's son, Jonathan, who becomes David's friend, and not the king himself.

David proves to be a highly successful soldier, and is even honoured with the hand of Saul's daughter in marriage. The king, however, grows jealous, and makes plans for killing David. Jonathan, however, remains loyal to his " covenant-friend " and finally enables him to escape. Most of the remaining chapters in I Samuel are occupied with the story of Saul's unsuccessful efforts to destroy his rival, and in two instances we have the record of David's chivalrous conduct in sparing Saul's life when he had the king at his mercy (chs. xxiv, xxvi). There are other incidents; David saves the city of Keilah from a Philistine attack, and deals with a wealthy farmer named Nabal. All this time he is gathering round him a band of outlaws, and moving from one desert stronghold to another. Finally (ch. xxvii) he takes refuge with Achish, king of Gath, one of the inland Philistine towns. Achish assigns to him the city of Ziklag, from which David conducts plundering raids to the south, persuading Achish that he is attacking Judahite cities.

This is the situation when the Philistines make their final attack on Saul, and the other Philistine chiefs compel Achish to dismiss David from his ranks (xxix). Saul, in his despair, consults the famous witch of Endor, who has communication with the spirits of the dead. She calls up the ghost of Samuel, who tells Saul that on the next day he will be defeated and killed (ch. xxviii). Meanwhile, David has returned to Ziklag, and found that the city had been sacked by Amalekites. He pursues the raiders, overtakes, and destroys them, recovering all the spoil they have carried off (ch. xxx). Finally, ch. xxxi records the defeat and death of Saul.

The story is told with great dramatic power, and forms one of the best monuments of Hebrew narrative prose. It is direct and simple, with plenty of detail but none of it unnecessary. The narrative moves straight forward and there is no time for the reader to grow weary; there is no meaningless verbiage. The whole forms a model of historical narrative.

With II Samuel we enter on a section which is almost certainly based on contemporary records, and quite probably contains detailed extracts from them. Chs. i-iv may be regarded as introductory since they give us the process by which David became king of all Israel. The section opens with David's reaction to the death of Saul and Jonathan. Information is brought by an Amalekite, who claims (falsely, to judge from I Sam. xxxi, 4) to have killed Saul at the king's request. Instead of a reward he meets with immediate death himself. Then follows David's lament over the dead king and Jonathan. It is one of the most touching poems in all literature, written for the most part in the characteristic Hebrew dirge form. Nowhere do we see David to better advantage. His grief over Jonathan's death is intelligible, but Saul has been for many years his deadly enemy. Yet with death all this is forgotten, and only the greatness of Saul is left in David's mind.

The next three chapters appear to come from contemporary sources, and describe the events which led to the complete union of Israel. David is left in the south, undisturbed by the Philistines, who have once more occupied the country north of Jerusalem. A feeble son of Saul's, Eshbaal[1] still maintains some hold to the east of the Jordan, but he is entirely dependent on his father's chief soldier, Abner. A quarrel between Abner and Eshbaal leads the former to make terms with David, but he falls to the jealousy of Joab, David's most powerful officer. Seven years after the death of Saul, Eshbaal is murdered, and David becomes the sole king of all Israel.

In ch. v, 4 we have the formula which stands at the head of each account of a reign. David's forty years are reckoned from the death of Saul, when he became king over the south. We have next an account of his main conquests and achievements. First comes the capture of Jerusalem (v. 6-9). The narrative here is obscure owing to textual corruption, but by comparing

---

[1] He is called Ishbosheth in II Sam., but his name is correctly given in 1 Chron. viii. 30, ix. 39.

the account in I Chron. xi, 4-8 we can see that Joab, followed by his men, scrambled up the tunnel which brought water from the Virgin's spring into the heart of the city.

Battles with the Philistines follow (v. 17-25). These are located in the Jerusalem area, and may have preceded the capture of that city. It is curious that his other wars against this enemy are passed over with slight reference, though they included the expulsion of the Philistines from the fertile plain of Esdraelon and even the occupation of Bethshan. But the compiler is keenly interested in religious matters, and it looks almost as if he had recorded the capture of Jerusalem in order to describe the removal of the Ark to the city which was to be its home as long as the monarchy lasted.

The establishment of the Ark in Jerusalem is given to us in ch. vi, and is followed by David's plan for building a temple (ch. vii). Possibly these two chapters are derived from Temple records. Ch. viii tells of David's further conquests; their effect is to establish a ring of subject peoples all round his southern and eastern frontiers, while he protected himself on the northern side by treaty with the king of Hamath. The chapter closes with notes on the organisation of his military and civil services.

With ch. ix begins the long extract from the court annals. It is not primarily concerned with the military and political events of the reign, though these are mentioned and described where they are necessary. The real subject is the court and family life of David. It begins with his treatment of Meribaal[1] the son of Jonathan. This is followed by the story of David's sin with Bathsheba (xi, 2-xii, 25). It is placed in the historical setting of war against Ammon and the Syrians of the north-east (x, 1-xi, 1, xii, 26-31). The remainder of the section is devoted to a detailed account of two rebellions against David, that of Absalom (chs. xiii-xix) and that of Sheba (ch. xx). Incidentally we gather that the union between Israel and Judah was by no means firmly established.

The last four chapters of II Samuel present us with a rather haphazard collection of varied material which the compiler may have gathered from other sources than those on

[1] Again a name has been distorted in Samuel, but the true form still appears in I Chron. viii. 34 and ix. 40. The change to Ishbosheth and Mephibosheth was probably made because the very name of Baal was detested by orthodox Jews, and replaced by " bosheth," which means " shame " or " a shameful thing."

which he has hitherto relied, or had omitted as interfering with the main course of his narrative. The latter suggestion seems to be the more probable, since there are sections which may well have been drawn from official documents of David's reign. The chief divisions are :

xxi, 1-14.   The vengeance taken by David on Saul's family for wrong done by Saul to Gibeon. It includes the touching story of Rizpah.

xxi, 15-22.   Exploits performed by some of David's heroes, chiefly in wars against the Philistines. It is curious to note that the slaughter of Goliath is here attributed to Elhanan and not to David (v. 19). This has so puzzled our translators that they have inserted the words " brother of " before " Goliath," with no justification from the Hebrew text. The problem was felt even by the compiler of Chronicles, who invented a certain Lahmi as Goliath's brother.

xxii.   A song of thanksgiving and triumph, also found as Ps. xviii. There is a widespread feeling, however, that it really comes from a later period, probably near the end of the monarchy. In substance it is not unsuited to David's position, and that may account for its inclusion here.

xxiii, 1-7.   Another hymn ascribed to David. It is much easier to accept the Davidic authorship of this Psalm than that of ch. xxii, even though its poetic quality does not rise to the height of the dirges ascribed to David in the earlier chapters of the book.

xxiii, 8-39.   A list of David's mighty men," with occasional notes on their exploits. As already noted, this list has every appearance of being taken from the official records of the king's reign.

xxiv.   David's sin in taking a census, with its consequences. Here we have a passage which in a sense belongs to the history of the Temple, and may have come from its archives. It explains the exact site on which the future Temple is to be built. There are several interesting features. The number of the people is a secret kept by God alone, unless He expressly tells men to share it. The effect of the punishment is to nullify the census; so many have perished that, once more, man is ignorant of the true figures.

So ends this book. We have no certain indication as to the date when it reached its present form, but we shall not greatly err if we ascribe it to the latter part of the seventh century.

It is almost certainly earlier than the exile, and at the same
time we have glimpses of the same spirit which we find in
Deuteronomy. There is a sense of the consecration of the
people to Yahweh, whose final symbol is to be the Temple.
That has not yet been built; David, like Moses, has been
allowed to see the promised land from afar, but not to enter
it himself. The completion of the great task is left to Solomon,
and his story begins with the Book of Kings.

Chapter IX

THE FORMER PROPHETS : I AND II KINGS

LIKE **Samuel, Kings** was originally a single book, but was
divided into two for practical convenience, each portion being
about the length of a moderate-sized scroll. It carries the story
of Israel down from the end of David's reign to the exile,
when Israel ceased for twenty-five centuries to have an independent political life in Palestine. It cannot have been completed before the exile, since its closing verses record an
event which took place in the year 560 B.C.

The sources employed by the compiler are fairly easy to
identify. First of all we have the royal annals, some of which
are used more fully than others. Solomon, in particular, has a
large section of the book devoted to him. At the end of nearly
every reign we find a reference to these royal annals, which,
presumably, were still supposed to be available for a reader
who wanted further information.

The second type of source is probably to be found in the
Temple records. Naturally, these begin with the building of
the Temple, and from time to time we meet with passages
which strongly suggest an ecclesiastical origin.

In the third place we have stories about the prophets. In
the earlier days of the monarchy these were probably handed
down orally, till they were collected by enthusiasts. It would
seem, however, that the narratives which deal with some of
the eighth- and seventh-century prophets were written during
the lifetime of the men whom they concerned. The three
whose names are best known to us all are Elijah, Elisha, and
Isaiah, though they are far from exhausting the list. We shall

meet with this type of literature again when we look at the "Later Prophets."

The Books of Kings fall into three parts :
  (a) Solomon (I Kings i-xi).
  (b) The Divided Kingdom (I Kings xii-II Kings xvii).
  (c) The later Kingdom of Judah (II Kings xviii-xxv).

(a) Chs. i, 1-ii, 11 record the last days of David and the events which led to Solomon's accession. He was one of David's younger sons, and had been born about two years after his father's last main war. The popular candidate was certainly an older son of David, Adonijah by name, but Solomon was supported by the royal bodyguard, the most efficient military force in the country, and had also the prestige given to him by his father's preference. The result was the complete collapse of the popular party (ch. i, 5-49).

Ch. ii tells us how Solomon dealt with the leaders of the popular party. It opens with David's last instructions to his son. Two men are to be destroyed, Joab and Shimei. The former had brought the guilt of blood on the crown by his treacherous murder of Abner and Amasa; the taint could be removed only by the blood of the slayer. Shimei had cursed David when he had fled from Absalom. The curse was still alive and active, and could be neutralised only by turning it on to the man who had uttered it. So Shimei, too, must die. These instructions are carried out in Solomon's own way. He dealt also with two other leaders of his opponents; Abiathar, being a priest, must not be killed, and so was banished to Anothoth, a small place some four miles north of Jerusalem. Adonijah asked for the youngest member of David's harem, and Solomon interpreted his request as a step towards a new rebellion—possibly correctly. Not till near the end of the reign was there any movement towards a "democratic" revolution which should replace the pure despotism of Solomon by the "limited monarchy" which was always the Israelite ideal polity.

In ch. iii we are told of incidents early in the young king's reign, particularly of his choosing "wisdom" in preference to wealth of long life, and of his skill as a judge. Ch. iv gives us the administrative districts into which the kingdom was divided. Their primary duty was to supply the court with its daily needs, but we may be sure that they were useful for every purpose of practical government. It is significant that

Judah is not mentioned in the list, and so, apparently, enjoyed preferential treatment. Vv. 20-34 add details of Solomon's expenditure and reputation.

With v. 1 begins the story of the Temple. The old friendship with Hiram of Tyre is maintained, and vast stores of timber are procured from Lebanon. Unskilled workmen, both in Lebanon and in Palestine, are provided from Israel by forced labour, a proceeding utterly revolting to the true Israelite spirit (vv. 13-18). Chs. vi and vii describe the actual building, and ch. viii the establishment of the Ark in it, followed by the great act of dedication.

Chs. ix and x are given to various incidents and details of the reign. We may notice especially Solomon's second vision (ix, 1-9), which strongly reminds us of the tone and style which we find in Deuteronomy, and so gives us a clue to the spirit in which the whole book is written. In ix, 26-28 there is a note telling us of Solomon's foreign sea-trade, and it seems clear that his voyages extended as far as India, if we may judge from the further reference in x, 22. And in x, 1-10 we read the dramatic story of the visit paid to Solomon by the Queen of Sheba.

Ch. xi tells the story of Solomon's decline. First place is given to his apostasy, for which his foreign wives are held responsible (vv. 1-13). Then two of the most important outlying dependencies were lost, Edom (xi, 14-22) and Syria (xi, 23-25). This must have reduced the royal income very considerably, for it deprives Solomon of that control over important trade routes which David had established. Finally came revolt in Israel itself, due, it seems, to discontent over the forced labour, and led by Jeroboam (xi, 26-40). It is most significant that Jeroboam was instigated by the prophet Ahijah, and that he found protection in Egypt. A new dynasty had arisen in that country during Solomon's reign, and the other two rebels had found refuge and support there. So Solomon died, leaving a terrible legacy of hostility abroad, discontent at home, and a bankrupt state.

(b) The results of Solomon's policy were seen at once. His son, Rehoboam, easily secured the adherence of Judah, but the north was another matter. Like David, he was compelled to make a " covenant " with the people on ascending the throne. Israel demanded, as a condition of this covenant, the abolition, or at least alleviation of the forced labour. He refused to agree, and at once the northern part of the kingdom broke away and chose Jeroboam as their king. The two realms never again achieved political unity (xii, 1-24).

From this point onwards, the historian has to keep the two kingdoms in view. His method is to describe the reign of a king of Judah (he begins with Rehoboam) and carry on the story of Judah, with the successive kings, indicating the accession year of each by the year in the reign of the contemporary Israelite king. When a king of Judah survives a king of Israel, the historian turns to the north, and repeats the process with the kings of Israel, till one survives the contemporary king of Judah. So, after telling the story of the secession and of Rehoboam's reign, he goes on to say that in the eighteenth year of Jeroboam, Abijam, the son of Jeroboam, began to reign over Judah. In Jeroboam's twentieth year, Asa became king of Judah. Asa survived Jeroboam, so the narrative continues to tell us that in Asa's second year, Nadab, son of Jeroboam became king of Israel, and continues the northern line till after the death of Asa. In this way he keeps a fairly steady synchronism between the two kingdoms, drawing on the annals of each in turn.

There are regular formulae for the beginning and end of each reign. First comes the synchronistic note, then in some cases the mother of a southern king is mentioned. The length of the reign is then given, and a judgment is passed on the moral and religious character of the reign. It would seem that the criterion is largely ritual; a king who worshipped other gods than Yahweh is at once condemned,, but a really good king must see that sacrifice is offered only in Jerusalem, and not at the old local sanctuaries, the "high places." Thus all the kings of Israel are condemned because they maintained the schismatic worship of Bethel. Any who, like Ahab, admitted other gods are still more strongly attacked. Eight of the southern kings are commended, though the approval is sometimes qualified by the statement that they did not suppress the "high places." Men like Hezekiah and Josiah who definitely tried to concentrate sacrifice in Jerusalem earn the highest commendation. Once again we have a clear indication of the compiler's outlook and purpose. He is not trying to write political history, but to present a record of the spiritual life of Israel during the monarchy; political events are incidental.

The first reign to be recorded in any detail is that of Jeroboam (xii, 20-xiv, 20). The compiler shows at once his interest in religious matters. A large part of the section is occupied with the establisment of sanctuaries at Bethel and Dan, together with the general organisation of the priesthood. There is reason to suspect that these shrines had long been in existence; it was Jeroboam who gave them national significance. Naturally, from the Deuteronomic point of view, they were schismatic, if not heretical. The " calf " (more properly a bull) was almost certainly held to be a symbol of Yahweh. We remember that in Ex. xxxii Aaron makes a similar image, declaring it to be the God who had brought Israel out of Egypt (Ex. xxxii, 4).

We note also the prominence given to prophets all through this narrative. The secession is instigated by Ahijah. Rehoboam's attempt to recover the north is checked by Shemaiah (I Kings xii, 22-24). Incidentally we may remark that some of the external evidence suggests that his efforts were not wholly unsuccessful, and that an Egyptian king, Shishak (or Sheshonk) came to the help of his *protégé*, Jeroboam. In ch. xiii an unnamed prophet comes from Judah, denounces the new cult, and disobeys his instructions, with fatal results to himself. This is clearly the sort of story current in Israel about the prophets, and it has a certain crudity which stamps it as an early tradition. Ahijah appears once more, this time as an old man whose sight had failed. Jeroboam's wife had gone to consult him for her son Abijah, and this prophet, in spite of the part he had played earlier, has nothing but condemnation for Jeroboam's religious policy (xiv, 1-18). His dynasty shall not last (xiv, 14); in fact no one family held the throne of the north for more than four generations.

The compiler now turns to the south, and gives us the record of Rehoboam's reign. Though Judah does not worship Yahweh in the form of a bull, the king and people still maintain the old local shrines, the " high places," and for this they are condemned. The most striking event is the Egyptian invasion, which stripped Jerusalem of the golden splendour with which Solomon had adorned the city (xiv, 25-28). So short-lived was the glory of Solomon.

Rehoboam died before Jeroboam, so the narrative continues with the southern kingdom, where Abijam succeeded his father. His was a short reign, uneventful from the compiler's

point of view, and we have only some theological reflections
(I Kings xv, 1-8). Jeroboam was still living, when Asa came
to the throne. He is the first king of Judah to be commended,
though with the reservation that the " high places " were still
maintained. He did, however, put an end to such idolatrous
worship as existed in Judah, even though his own mother was
implicated in it. He also suppressed the male prostitutes who
were to be found in many sanctuaries among the Semitic
peoples (cf. xiv, 24). The only other point worth noticing is
the success of Israel in the constant border warfare between
the two kingdoms. Asa was reduced to calling in the king of
Damascus, the new state founded during the reign of Solomon.
This step had serious consequences for Israel and, ultimately,
for Judah, but for the time the pressure on the south was
relieved.

Asa had a long reign, and attention is now turned to Israel.
Jeroboam's son, Nadab was assassinated by a certain Baasha
after a short reign (xv, 25-32). Baasha in turn was condemned
by a prophet named Jehu, but maintained his position for
twenty-four years (xv, 33-xvi, 7). His son, Elah, however, was
killed in a palace revolution by Zimri, and all the house of
Baasha exterminated (xvi, 8-14). But Zimri's reign lasted only
seven days; Israelite forces were besieging Gibbethon, a town
in the foothills probably held by Philistines. The commander
of the troops there, Omri, promptly made his way to Shechem,
and Zimri, in despair, committed suicide. Omri still had to
fight for the kingdom against a rival named Tibni, but was
successful in the end (xvi, 15-22).

Omri was the greatest of the northern kings, but he is dismissed in six verses (xvi, 23-28). The one act of his reign
here recorded is the building of Samaria as his new capital.
But he was so important a king that for long afterwards his
country was known in Mesopotamia as " the land of Omri."
His conquest of Moab, too, is recorded by the Moabites themselves, and he was closely allied to the Phoenicians. It is clear
that he went far towards restoring the old limits of the
Davidic kingdom; even Judah appears to have been a subordinate ally.

Omri's son, Ahab, was also a strong man, and took a leading
part in the movement which resisted the invasions of Assyria.
More space is given to his reign by the historian than to any
other king since Solomon; even Hezekiah receives only half

as much notice. This is not due to Ahab's own qualities, but to the appearance of a far greater man, one of the grandest figures in the Old Testament. This was Elijah, who appears as a leading actor in every event recorded in this reign except in the story of the king's death. Elijah stood for the genuine Israelite tradition in religion and in social life; to the ancient Hebrew the two were inseparable. The narrative makes it clear that his quarrel was less with Ahab than with the Phoenician queen, Jezebel. She attempted to introduce the Baal of Sidon as the chief god of Israel, and she refused to recognise the Israelite insistence on the rights of the subject against the monarch.

The religious struggle begins with a great drought of three years produced and controlled by the prophet. His personal experiences during that time are described (xvii). The drought ends with the great trial scene on Mt. Carmel, where the authority of Yahweh in the land of Israel is finally vindicated. The closing act of challenge is the slaughter of the Baal priests; a god who could not protect or avenge his sacred persons had no standing in the country (xviii). The state of high ecstatic tension passes, Elijah loses his nerve for the time, and flees to the far south from Jezebel's fury. He repairs to the "mountain of God," Horeb, where Moses had first met Yahweh, and where the nation of Israel had been born. There he receives a new commission, the appointment of three men who are to carry on his work. It seems that he dealt only with one directly; the other two received their commission from his successor, Elisha. This section of the "Acts of Elijah" ends with ch. xix.

Ch. xx reverts to political, or rather military history. Benhadad of Damascus attacks Samaria, and is defeated in two decisive battles. Instead of using his advantage to crush Damascus, Ahab prefers to ally himself with the Syrian king; possibly he already foresaw the great Assyrian advance (ch. xx). That came in 853 B.C., the first certain date in Israelite history. Curiously enough, the great battle at Karkar is not mentioned in the Bible; our knowledge of the most important battle in the history of the Israelite monarchy comes to us only from Assyrian sources. It did not interest the writer, for it had no bearing on the religious life of Israel.

In ch. xxi we have the last clash between Elijah and Jezebel. It is the matter of Naboth's vineyard. Here the Israelite prin-

E

ciple of the subject's rights is vindicated. Ahab's conduct is still consistent with the national tradition; he takes Naboth's No! as final. Jezebel insists that the king is an absolute despot, and gets the vineyard for the king. But it carries the taint of blood, and when Ahab takes possesssion of it he brings down that curse on himself and on his family. From then onwards the dynasty of Omri is doomed.

Ch. xxii, 1-40 records the death of Ahab. The narrative introduces a prophet who does not appear elsewhere, Micaiah the son of Imlah. The narrative is interesting and important for the history and understanding of prophecy before the age of Isaiah; Micaiah is both the ecstatic prophet and the seer. But he fails to convince the king, and Ahab goes to his death at Ramoth Gilead.

In the meantime Asa has died, and his son, Jehoshaphat, is now on the throne (xxii, 41-50). He is commended as his father had been, but little is here recorded of his reign, and the narrative turns back to the north. Ahab was succeeded by Ahaziah (I Kings xxii, 51-II Kings i, 18). The greater part of the passage is taken up with the story of Elijah calling down fire from heaven on the king's soldiers sent to arrest him. This is followed, in ch. ii, by the narrative of Elijah's departure from the scene of his labours, caught up in a fiery chariot and taken into heaven.

In the prophetic narratives Elisha now takes the place of Elijah. Jehoram has succeeded his brother Ahaziah, and is attempting to bring back the revolted Moabites to their allegiance. In spite of the prophet's intervention (which does, indeed, save the army from thirst and win a victory in the field), the expedition fails, owing to Mesha's action in sacrificing his eldest son (II Kings iii).

Chs. iv, 1-viii, 15 give us a selection from the " Acts of Elisha." They are too well known to require detailed study; suffice it to note that the prophet is usually on friendly terms with the court. There are passages which suggest tension, if not hostility; in II Kings iii, 13, for example, Elisha has no respect for the son of Jezebel. While kings are not named elsewhere, it may be assumed that those whom Elisha favoured belonged to the house of Jehu.

Before passing to an account of the prophetic revolution which destroyed the house of Ahab, the writer has to mention two kings of Judah who came to the throne during the reign

of Jehoram, king of Israel. These are Jehoram,, son of
Jehoshaphat (II Kings viii, 16-24), and his son Ahaziah (II
Kings viii, 25-29). Both are condemned by the compiler,
because they associated themselves with the house of Omri.
Jehoram married Athaliah, the sister of the northern king,
and both he and his son are said to have " walked in the way
of Ahab." We must not take this to mean that either tried to
establish the cult of the Phoenician Baal; their names, even
also that of Athaliah, show that Yahweh was still regarded
as the God of Israel and Judah.

In chs. ix and x we have the account of the great revolution
which settled for ever the conflict between Yahweh and Baal.
At the instigation of Elisha, both Jehoram, king of Israel, and
Ahaziah, king of Judah, are assassinated, Jezebel is killed, and
all the kin of Ahab massacred. This may be claimed as the
vengeance of Israel for the blood of Naboth, but a century
later it was strongly condemned by Hosea, a prophet who
certainly had no sympathy with the Baal cult (Hos. i, 4).
While this section may come from the official annals of the
kingdom, it has certainly been coloured by the prophetic
tradition. It is not, however, strictly a prophetic story, for
Elisha plays no part in it after giving instructions for the
anointing of Jehu.

On the political side, the revolution had unpleasant results.
We learn from Assyrian sources that Jehu deserted the alliance
with the other states in that area, which had successfully
resisted Shalmaneser III. The first effect was the loss of all the
eastern territory, which was occupied by the Syrians, under
their vigorous king, Hazael. This is recorded for us in II
Kings x, 32f. Later, the collapse of the alliance led to the
advance of Assyria, and to the subjugation of all the west to
the great Mesopotamia power.

In ch. xi we turn back to events in Judah. The death of
Ahaziah did not mean the immediate success of the reforming
party. His mother, Athaliah, seized the throne, and, in oriental
fashion, murdered all her son's family. One child, however,
escaped, and six years later was placed on the throne by a
coup d'état. Athaliah was killed, but there was no such general
slaughter as had accompanied the revolution in the north. It
is worth noting that in Judah there is no mention of the
prophets; it is the priest Jehoiada who carries the matter
through. The full details which are given suggest that this

record is taken either from the royal annals or from the archives of the Temple.

Ch. xii gives us an account of events in the reign of Joash. He is said to have behaved well as long as Jehoiada lived, and to have repaired the Temple, using contributions made by Israel and placed in a special chest. This passage (xii, 4-16) clearly comes from the Temple records. The only other event assigned in this book to the reign of Joash is the attack made by Hazael on Judah. The king of Damascus seems to have occupied a large part of western Palestine, for his objectives even included Gath, on the Judah-Philistine border.

The narrative now turns back to the north, where Jehoahaz, son of Jehu (xiii, 1-9) was followed by his own son, Joash (xiii, 10-13). Both are condemned by the compiler, since both maintained the northern sanctuaries, but the sentence does not seem to be as severe as that passed on the house of Omri. It was during the reign of Jehoahaz that Israel began to recover from the political weakness which had followed the accession of Jehu. The real reason seems to have been a general movement westwards by Assyria, which reduced Damascus to impotence late in the ninth century B.C. The writer has made no mention of this, since Judah had not yet come into direct contact with Assyria.

Political history is interrupted here to tell the story of Elisha's death (xiii, 14-21). It introduces the recovery of Israel under Joash, and xiii, 22-25 appear to have been written before the last troubles of Samaria. Perhaps they are taken from the annals of Joash; certainly they seem to have a northern origin, for there is no hint of condemnation on the king for maintaining the sanctuaries at Bethel and Dan.

Recovery in the north was accompanied by recovery in the south. Amaziah, who succeeded Joash in Jerusalem, conquered Edom once more, but his pride led him to challenge Joash, king of Israel. The result was the complete defeat of Judah, and the spoiling of Jerusalem. Fifteen years after the death of Joash, Amaziah was assassinated, and succeeded by his young son Azariah (xiv, 1-22).

Meanwhile the throne of the north was occupied by the most successful of all the Israelite kings since Solomon. This was Jeroboam II, son of Joash, and the notice we have in II Kings xiv, 23-29, like that of Jehoahaz in xiii, 5, comes from a northern source and is clearly earlier than the fall of Samaria. While we have fewer quotations from the northern annals than from the southern, it seems clear that both adopted the same general form and tone. The chief difference lay in the attitude of the two realms towards the religious establishment of Jeroboam I, but both clung to a belief in Yahweh as the one God of Israel, and a confidence that He would never allow his chosen people to be destroyed. He might punish them for their sin, but his promise to Abraham must be eternally valid.

Azariah, elsewhere called Uzziah, is one of the kings who are said to have done that which was right in the eyes of Yahweh, except for the fact that the local sanctuaries, the " high places," were left undisturbed. He became a leper, and for the last years of his life his son, Jotham, acted as regent (xv, 1-7).

Jeroboam died before Azariah; he was followed by his son Zechariah, and the collapse of the north began. Repeated revolutions exhausted the strength of the government; after Jeroboam II only one northern king handed on the throne to a son. At the same time it is clear from the contemporary prophets that a social and economic change had taken place. Free peasant proprietors of the Naboth type had been almost eliminated, and the large estates were cultivated by something very like serf labour. The moral vigour of the nation was sapped, and when a serious enemy appeared, three kings followed in quick succession, Zechariah, son of Jeroboam (xv, 8-12), Shallum (xv, 13-16) and Menahem (xv, 17-21). The last named retained his throne, largely with the help of Tiglath-pileser, to whom he paid tribute, and he was followed by his son, Pekahiah (xv, 23-26). Again the king met with a violent death, and his reign ended with the first great invasion of Tiglath-pileser, who took from Israel all her territory except a small district round Samaria, in the north of the central hill country (xv, 27-31). We know from Assyrian sources that the great king organised the captured districts as provinces, and the Biblical record tells us that he deported their population to Mesopotamia.

In Judah, Azariah was succeeded by Jotham, who continued his father's policy (xv, 32-38). He was faced with a coalition between Pekah and Rezin, king of Damascus. It appears that they were trying to revive the old coalition which had successfully resisted Assyria a century earlier, and hoped to force Judah into the alliance. In this they failed; the spirit of the population had been broken by the economic and social changes which had taken place between Ahab and Pekah. Judah, too, was determined to stand aloof, and so escaped destruction for another hundred and fifty years. Judah was, in fact, the only state in the west which survived Assyria; all the rest had disappeared and been absorbed in the great Mesopotamian empire.

With Ahaz (ch. xvi) we enter a period in which events are more fully recorded. The northern allies were for a time successful, and Edom recovered her liberty; Jerusalem itself was seriously threatened. In this extremity, Ahaz appealed to Tiglath-pileser, and offered to become a vassal of his if he would protect him against the allies. The Assyrian king needed little persuasion, and was soon in the west. Ahaz (his full name was Jehoahaz, but it may be conjectured that pious Jews refused to give him a name in which the element Yahweh was to be found) went to Damascus, where Tiglath-pileser made his headquarters while he settled his new provinces, and there saw an altar, probably of an Assyrian pattern. He ordered a similar altar to be set up in Jerusalem. This probably means that, as a token of submission to Assyria, he had to establish the cult of an Assyrian god alongside that of Yahweh. This was not his only religious offence; the record accuses him of sacrificing his eldest son, possibly during the Syro-Ephraimite attack on Jerusalem.[1] Only one other king of Judah, Manasseh, is so fiercely condemned as is Ahaz.

The Assyrian settlement had left a small territory round Samaria under a king named Hoshea (xvii, 1-6). But he rebelled, Tiglath-pileser deposed and imprisoned him; after a three years' seige, Samaria itself was captured, and the people were deported to north-eastern Mesopotamia, where they simply merged with the population already there.

The writer then gives the reason for this calamity. It is due to the manifold sins of Israel, especially their maintenance of the illegitimate cults (xvii, 7-23). This is written from the Deuteronomic point of view, which held that Jerusalem was the only spot where true sacrifice could be offered to Yahweh. Whatever else, good or bad, the kings of Israel had done or

[1] We may compare the action of Mesha, king of Moab, in similar straits, II Kings iii. 27).

not done, they had never recognised the spiritual priority of Jerusalem, and had never abandoned the cults established by Jeroboam I. So they deserved their end.

Samaria itself was repopulated by drafts from various parts of the Assyrian empire (xvii, 24-41). They brought with them, naturally, their own gods. But they were troubled with lions (v. 25), and ascribed their calamities to the anger of the native deity. So a priest was brought back from Assyria to teach them how Yahweh should be worshipped. They carried out the instructions, but did not abandon their old national gods, and even down to the time of the writer this syncretistic form of religion retained its hold in the north. While the later Samaritans were not to be charged with this form of apostasy, the taint of ancient days still clung to them after centuries, and made easy the breach between the two groups which were formed after the exile.

Now we come to the third section of the Books of Kings, that which deals with Judah alone. Hezekiah, the son of Ahaz (xviii-xx) is the first king since David who wins unqualified approval from the compiler. The reason is that he organised a complete reform of religion, sweeping away all that was offensive in the eyes of the stricter Jews. The local sanctuaries were suppressed, their sacred stones and poles destroyed, and even the ancient snake shrine in Jerusalem abolished. Tradition had it that the object of worship there was the actual " seraph " which Moses had erected in the wilderness as a cure for the bites of the " seraphs " or " fiery serpents " which had attacked them there (Num. xxi, 9).

Inserted in the reign of Hezekiah is another brief statement of the fall of Samaria (xviii, 9-12). It comes clearly from a different source than the section xvii, 1-6, though the facts are the same, in the main. We do, however, get the impression from the earlier passage that Hosea was captured and deposed before the siege of Samaria began, while the later record indicates that he was on the throne till the fall of the city. The former of these two presentations is easier to fit into a chronological scheme. In ch. xviii the fall of Samaria is followed immediately by the great invasion of Sennacherib, which took place in 701 B.C. (vv. 13-16). The facts stated in this short statement tally exactly with the full account given by Sennacherib in his own inscriptions, though the Assyrian king goes into far more detail.

An unusual amount of space is given to Hezekiah. It is largely occupied with selections from a collection of " Acts of Isaiah "; the prophet is the outstanding figure throughout. The same collection was used by the compiler of the Book of Isaiah, in chs. xxxvi-xxxix, though the two do not wholly overlap. In Kings there are four main excerpts. We have the summons of Rabshakeh (xviii, 17-xix, 8), followed by a reference to the abortive attempt by the Egyptian king to repel Sennacherib (xix, 9). Then a second demand, this time by letter to Hezekiah; presumably there is now no hope of rescue. The king prays in the Temple, and Isaiah is sent to give him a message of deliverance. This includes a long prophetic poem (xix, 21-28), a prediction of disaster (xix, 29-34), and an account of the slaughter inflicted by Yahweh on the Assyrian forces. Probably this was an attack of bubonic plague; the Greek historian Herodotus heard a tradition of an Assyrian disaster in this region, where " mice " were concerned, and in such circumstances we always suspect plague-rats.

The third incident is the story of Hezekiah's sickness and recovery (xx, 1-11), followed by the embassy of Merodach-baladan (in Babylonian Marduk-appal-iddina) to Hezekiah (xx, 12-19). It is clear that the compiler has not placed his events in chronological order. Marduk-appal-iddina was the organiser of the general revolt against Sennacherib; he was defeated and disappeared before Sennacherib made his great expedition into Palestine.

Hezekiah was succeeded by his son, Manasseh (xxi, 1-18). The record of his reign consists almost entirely of the sins he committed. So heinous were they that the writer attributes to them the final destruction of the Jewish state. But it must be remembered that he was always a vassal of the Assyrian crown, and was probably compelled to introduce Assyrian cults and methods into his religious establishment. Ahaz had been in the same position, and the reforms of Hezekiah may well have been connected with his revolt against Sennacherib. It is impossible to draw a clear line of demarcation between religion and politics in the ancient world. With the reduction of Judah to the Assyrian authority, it is more than likely that Mesopotamian elements were reintroduced, though Hezekiah himself may not have gone so far as his son.

After a brief interlude formed by the reign of Amon (xviii, 19-26), Josiah came to the throne as a child of eight. His reign is one of the most important in the religious history of Israel and Judah. During his minority the Temple fabric fell into disrepair, and one of his first acts when he assumed the government was to restore it. As the work was being carried out, a book of the Law was found. This is unusually identified with Deuteronomy, or a great part of it, and the date of the discovery, 621 B.C., is generally regarded as a landmark in religious history. Then, for the first time, the law of the single altar was fully recognised and operative in Israel. On the advice of the prophetess Huldah, a complete reform was carried out. Like Hezekiah, Josiah probably had politics as well as religion on his mind. His reign coincided with the fall of Assyria, and he was free to do as he pleased in dealing with the Jerusalem cult. The story of the reform is told in xxii, 8-xxiii, 20, and culminated in a great celebration of the Passover. If observed at all, this had, so it seems, been a domestic festival, the victim being killed at the local "high place," but prepared and eaten in the worshipper's own home. Now the whole process was carried out in Jerusalem, and Josiah's celebration formed the model for the post-exilic practice.

The collapse of Assyria is well illustrated by the fact that Josiah could carry his reform well into the old Assyrian provinces; we find Samaria mentioned in xxiii, 19, and special attention is given to the desecration of the sanctuary at Bethel (xxiii, 15-18). The detailed list of the cult-objects suppressed or destroyed in Jerusalem itself makes us feel that under Manasseh the Temple had become a sort of religious museum, where forms of worship from many countries had been represented. Josiah was, from the religious point of view, the ideal king, and, in a sense, may be regarded as the second founder of Judaism, since even the work of Ezra was based on what this king had done.

It was the political aspect of the reform which led to Josiah's ruin. Assyria was attacked by Babylonians and Medes. The city of Asshur fell in 614 B.C., and Nineveh itself in 612. Gradually the Assyrians were forced back to the north-west, and in 610 the allies captured the city of Haran. There our detailed information ceases, but there is reason to believe that the struggle was carried on from Carchemish, still further to the north-west. From the start of the war, in 616 B.C., the Egyptian king, Necho, had led an army into Mesopotamia, and done his best to help the falling Assyrian power[1]; his expeditions normally lasted about three months, and certainly delayed the final victory of Babylon.

In the year 608 B.C., Josiah was implicated. The record in II Kings xxiii, 29-30 simply states that he went to Megiddo to meet Necho, " and when he saw him, he put him to death." The simple fact is that Necho was pro-Assyrian and Josiah anti-Assyrian, and might be a serious danger to the Pharoah's communications. So Josiah had to die.

The story of independent Judah is nearly finished. A popular movement placed Josiah's second son, Jehoahaz, on the throne. But, apparently on his return from Mesopotamia, Necho deposed him and installed his older brother, Jehoiakim, as a vassal of Egypt (xxiii, 31-35). But Necho was completely overthrown at Carchemish in 605 B.C.; this is one of the decisive battles in history, for Egypt was never again to make a bid for world supremacy, and Assyria vanished for ever. Nebuchadrezzar,[2] the young king who had won the victory at Carchemish in the last year of his father's life, invaded Palestine, and Jehoiakim was forced to change his allegiance. Three years later he proved unfaithful, and a Babylonian army marched against Jerusalem. Jehoiakim died before Jerusalem was taken, but three months later his young son Jehoiachin was compelled to surrender at the conqueror's discretion. The young king was carried captive to Babylon, together with many of the more prominent people and the best craftsmen in Judah; Ezekiel was among them, and, possibly, the writer of Pss. xlii-xliii. A third son of Josiah, Zedekiah by name, was substituted for his nephew (xxiii, 36-xxiv, 17).

The reign of Zedekiah contained only one event which seemed important to the historian; that was the fall of Jerusalem, and it outweighed everything else that he had written. The Jewish king rebelled, Jerusalem was besieged, Zedekiah escaped but was pursued and captured. He was taken to Riblah, and compelled to witness the execution of his sons before his own eyes were put out. Then he was carried to Babylon to die. Jerusalem was stripped of everything valuable, its walls broken

---

[1] In II Kings xxiii. 29 a preposition is commonly misread. We know from Babylonian records that Necho did not go up *against* the king of Assyria, but to support him.

[2] His name is misspelt as Nebuchadnezzar in most parts of our Bible, but the correct form, corresponding to the Babylonian Nabu-kudurri-usur, appears in some chapters of Jeremiah and in Ezekiel.

down, the Temple burnt, and the inhabitants taken to Babylonia. Only a few peasants were left in the country to cultivate the soil (xxiv, 18-xxv, 21).

Even so, Judah's sufferings were not ended. Judah was organised as a province, and a certain Gedaliah was placed in charge of it. He was a member of an old noble Jewish family, and a man of high character and chivalrous disposition. It seems that he had already done much to give a new life to his humble people, when he was assassinated by a scion of the royal house named Ishmael. Gedaliah's bodyguard fled to Egypt, fearing Babylonian vengeance, and some of them may been the ancestors of that strange Jewish community which we find at Elephantine in the fifth century B.C. But in Judah itself there was little left that could revive or carry on a national life (xxv, 22-26).

The book ends with a note telling us that after thirty-seven years of captivity, Jehoiachin was released from prison by Evilmerodach (Babylonian Amel-marduk), and given a position at court. Apparently he was allowed to marry, for we hear of a grandson who played an important part in the re-establishment of the Jews after the exile (xxv, 27-30).

We have much fuller accounts of the last days elsewhere in the Old Testament. Lamentations ii and iv give us a vivid picture of the horrors endured during the final siege, and Lam. i shows us something of the desolate state in which Jerusalem lay throughout the exile. In the prophetic narratives concerning Jeremiah we have a fairly extensive account of events which took place in the reign of Zedekiah, or at least in its last years. The greater part of Jer. xxxiv-xlv is concerned with events during and after the revolt of Zedekiah. Probably the compiler had no access to this collection of the "Acts of Jeremiah." The prophet himself, together with his secretary, Baruch (to whom, probably, we owe the narratives) were taken to Egypt after the murder of Gedaliah. The compiler of Kings in its final form seems to have done his work in Babylonia, though the frequent references to the royal annals suggests that a large part was completed while these and other records were still available, that is, before the exile.

In the books of Samuel to Kings we have a complete record of a nation's history, so far as it was a fairly united and independent political entity. It deserves a closer study from the professional historian's point of view than it has generally received. It shows us in compact form the kind of situation which makes a national state possible, and the conditions which must be fulfilled if that state is to maintain a successful existence. It makes it clear that there are certain laws of personality, as immutable as those of the physical world, which must be taken into account. These are set before the reader as the will of God, and they apply both to man's relations with Him and to his dealings with his fellows. If they are disregarded, sooner or later the great social and political experiment will fail, and it will end in utter ruin. Every page of world history attests and supports the principles which this record enunciates for us.

CHAPTER X

THE LATER PROPHETS: THE STRUCTURE OF THE BOOKS AND THE GENERAL TEACHING OF THE PROPHETS

In the Jewish scriptures the collection of the Later Prophets includes four volumes: Isaiah, Jeremiah, Ezekiel, The Twelve. These latter are: Hosea, Joel, Amos, Obadiah, Jonah, Micah, Nahum, Habakkuk, Zephaniah, Haggai, Zechariah, Malachi. We are apt to call the first three "major" and the last twelve "minor," but the twelve include some which are of the first importance, especially Hosea and Amos; Haggai and Zechariah, too, throw light on the period of the return from exile, which is otherwise most obscure.

Now when we read these books, we become conscious of their varied nature. In them there is a great deal of poetry; there is also a large amount of prose. This is of two kinds; in the one the prophet recounts his own experiences, and in the other a third party describes events in his life. We have already noted that collections of the last type were freely used by the compilers of the "Former Prophets."

We have, then, three types of writing. Let us look first at that which has come down to us in verse form. We soon see that it consists very largely of short, vigorous pieces, each dealing with a single subject; often introduced with the words: "Thus saith the LORD." This might be rendered

" Thus said . . ." if we wished to bring out the exact force of the tense used. At the end we frequently find the phrase, " saith the LORD." This looks in English very much like the other, but in Hebrew it is totally different. It implies that what has gone before is something which has been received by the prophet direct from God, and is a claim, or a certificate, of divine inspiration ; it probably indicates that the words repeated have been actually heard by the prophet while under the influence of his abnormal condition (*cf.* p. 52).

These short prophetic pieces occur as a rule in fairly long sections. We have a comparatively short one in Isaiah i. Vv. 2-3 are an appeal to heaven and earth to testify that Yahweh has found Israel to be rebellious or indifferent to Him. Then in vv. 4-9 there is a pathetic description of a desolate land, nearly as bad as ruined Sodom and Gomorrah. These two names stand at the head of the next piece, which may go as far as v. 20. But in v. 9 it is the ruined state of the two cities which the prophet laments, while in v 10 he is thinking of their wickedness, and the latter passage is a denunciation of sacrifice as practised in Israel, followed by an appeal for a moral reformation. V. 20 ends with a variation of the " saith the LORD " phrase : " For the mouth of the LORD has spoken." We have another break at the end of v. 23.

We cannot resist the impression that in this and many other instances we have collections of prophetic utterances. We do not know who the collectors were, and we can guess at their methods only from a study of the text. But it seems possible that the words spoken by the prophet were handed down from mouth to mouth till at last they were written by some enthusiast, possibly on bits of broken pottery like the famous Lachish letters. Other enthusiasts would collect them, and if such a man found a piece of special value, he might not to be too particular as to the prophet who first uttered it. It was the word of God, and the human channel was comparatively unimportant. So several times we find the same utterance included in collections bearing the names of different prophets. In other places we sometimes suspect that a particular " oracle " was not given through the prophet to whom the collection is ascribed. These doubtful cases are most frequent at the end of a collection.

Collectors have interesting habits. They sometimes put together pieces which had a common phrase, even if they did not deal with the same subject; we had an instance in Isaiah i, where one oracle ended with Sodom and Gomorrah, and the next, which has no other connection with the first, begins with the same names. What they most liked, however, was to collect oracles which threatened foreign nations. Each of the larger books has a section of this kind, and **Amos** begins with one. The little book of Obadiah appears to be solely a collection of utterances against Edom; two or more of these are found again in the Edom collection in Jeremiah.

We turn now to the prose portions in which the prophet himself is speaking. These passages nearly always give the substance of some oracle, though in longer form; Hebrew prose is not so crisp as its poetry. There is some of this in Isaiah and a good deal in Jeremiah, while the greater part of Ezekiel is in this form. Among the Twelve there is one such passage in Hosea (ch. iii), and accounts of several visions in Amos. Haggai may have been originally written in the first person, though in its present form it belongs to the next group. Zechariah i-viii, xi, 4-16 are spoken by the prophet in his own person and passages in xii-xiv are in prose, though the prophet does not speak of himself.

At times we get the impression that these prose utterances are themselves collections. Their style and tone are so different from those of the poetic oracles that we can hardly suppose they were verbatim recollections of what a prophet had said, handed down by word of mouth. They have the appearance of artistic literary productions, and may have been written or dictated by the prophet himself. In Jeremiah xxxvi we have a detailed account of the way in which Jeremiah, unable to speak in public, arranged for the preservation of his words in book form; Baruch is told to write down all that the prophet had said from the beginning of his ministry. The date is 605 B.C., the year of Carchemish, and it is significant that nearly all the passages of this type in **Jeremiah** can be assigned to dates earlier than this. Further, when a prophet describes his call, it is always in prose, though in one case, that of Amos, it is included in a narrative due to a biographer.

One interesting feature of this group of material is that passages are often dated. Thus we have an exact date in Isaiah vi, 1 and viii, 1. Dates are fairly common in Jeremiah and in Ezekiel. The prophetic material which follows does not always fit the same occasion and the dated verses may have been placed by the prophet at the head of small collections.

There are prose biographical passages in Isaiah, especially at the end of the book, and considerable sections in Jeremiah. Hos. i belongs to this class, and so does Am. vii, 10-17. The book of Jonah (except for the Psalm in ch. ii) is entirely descriptive; the only words of prophecy in it are those which announce the coming doom of Nineveh.

The three types have been combined by compilers in different ways, and we can notice these when we come to look at the individual books.

At this point it may be useful to note that there are certain beliefs which are characteristic of the prophets as a group. Each has his own marked individuality, and each stresses certain special aspects of the general teaching, but there are points on which all would agree. We may especially observe the following:

(i) *Yahweh is the Lord of the physical world.* We find stories of creation in the folk-tales of many peoples. The making of the world is almost invariably ascribed to one or other of the gods; the rest may help or hinder or remain comparatively indifferent till the task is done. In the Semitic world there grew up elaborate myths, which have come to light in modern times. One of the best-known tells of war between the gods of light and the gods of darkness, and has become familiar to many of us in its Babylonian form. It tells of a female monster, Tiamat, and her male associate, Kingu, who threatened the other gods with destruction. They met in council, and one of them, Marduk by name, volunteered to meet the demons. He did so, and after destroying Tiamat, made the earth from her dismembered body. Other Mesopotamian peoples had a similar story, but with a different hero. Marduk was the patron god of Babylon; in the Assyrian form of the story the victory was won by Asshur, the national deity, and among the Sumerians the god Enlil played the leading part. Such a story may have been current in Israel, with Yahweh as the creator, but if so, it has almost disappeared. Nevertheless, the prophets, like all other true Israelites, believed that Yahweh was the creator of the universe.

(ii) *Yahweh is the Lord of History.* Every people, in a sense, believed that its god controlled its fortunes. If they displeased him, he might punish them by allowing their enemies to triumph over them, or by withholding the necessary rain from them. But he was not concerned with other nations, except in so far as they might be used to vindicate his power against his own subjects. On the other hand, the Israelite prophet had a real philosophy of history. He believed that the whole course of human life, even the great racial migrations, was subject to a vast plan in the mind of Yahweh, who controlled not only the fate of Israel, but that of every people in the world. Their claims for Yahweh, whom others saw as only the deity of a small Palestinian state, went far beyond those made by any other nation for its god.

(iii) *Yahweh is the Lord of universal morality.* As a rule, religion and ethics have little to do with one another. In most faiths, a god takes man's dealings with his fellows into account only when special appeal is made to the deity. Within his own people he may act as supreme judge in cases of dispute, but unless he is called in he does not concern himself with justice and injustice. The oath is a significant example of this feeling. A god will take no notice of a man who lies or fails to carry out his promises unless he has sworn an oath. That is to say, he has called on the god to punish him if he does not fulfil his promises or speaks falsely. The god will take vengeance, not for the moral offence, but for the insult to his person. Now the Hebrew prophet not only insisted that Yahweh need not be brought into a transaction; He could not be kept out of it. What is more, He was interested in actions which had no bearing on Israel, matters which, as men thought, were outside His province.

(iv) *Yahweh is the Lord of the end of things.* Just as every nation had its own theory of the way in which the world began, so it also speculated on the way in which it would end. In Israel there had long been an " eschatology," a doctrine of the last days. It was, naturally, highly patriotic; men believed that when the right time arrived, Yahweh himself would interfere, bring the present order to an end, and establish His own kingdom. Such a kingdom must mean the supremacy of His people; and at long last Israel would subdue all her enemies, and a reign of universal prosperity for them would be inaugurated. The prophets, too, had an eschatology, but it did not take the popular form. Yahweh would intervene, but His purpose would not be to exalt Israel, but to vindicate on her His moral principles. It was to be " a day of darkness, not a day of light," and the rotten state of the country would meet with its due reward at the hands of the one perfectly righteous God.

(v) *Yahweh is the special God of Israel.* The " covenant " which had brought them into being made Him their God and them His people. But that privilege brought with it responsibility. They were to be His instruments in bringing knowledge of Him to the world; if they failed there, they would be cast on one side, and their place taken by more effective agents.

(vi) *Yahweh's supreme demand was for righteousness, not for ritual.* There is a wide difference of opinion among Old Testament scholars as to the real attitude of the pre-exilic prophets to sacrifice. On the surface there are passages (e.g. Is. i, 10-17) which appear to denounce sacrifice in any form. On the other hand it is maintained that these passages mean only that sacrifice must not be made a substitute for moral conduct. Yahweh wants it, but it can be acceptable only if it is given by people whose lives conform to the ethical principles which He imposes on all men. The post-exilic prophets, from Ezekiel onwards, make it clear that sacrifice was an essential element in true religion, and that it must be offered in the right way and by the right persons.

When all these points are considered together, it will be realised that in all history there has never been a group of men who have exercised so profound an influence on human thinking. There have been outstanding individuals in many lands and in many faiths, but here we have a series of speakers, doing their work over a period of some four centuries, and maintaining doctrines which have gained wide acceptance, and dominate three of the world's great religions, Judaism, Christianity, and Islam.

CHAPTER XI

THE LATER PROPHETS : ISAIAH

ISAIAH lived and worked in the latter part of the eighth century B.C. His ministry seems to have begun about 740, some twenty years before the fall of Samaria, and the last datable utterances we have from him belong to the great invasion of Sennacherib in 701. He was a conspicuous figure, especially in the reign of Hezekiah, and played no small part in Israelite political life.

The book which bears his name contains writings of all the three types we have noted. Most of it consists of poetic oracles, which seem to have been gathered into smaller collections before being arranged in their present form. Prose in the first person is found in chs. vi, viii, 1-4, and many scholars think that " to Isaiah " in vii, 3 is a copyist's error for " to me "; this would cover all the verses that follow, down to v. 17, and add them to this short list. In xxi, 16, 17, too, we have a couple of prose verses in the first person.

Then we have prose in the third person, that is material in which someone else speaks of what the prophet did or said. These passages include a kind of editor's introduction to the whole book, and to some other collections of oracles. Ch. xx is also of this type, but it is mainly found in chs. xxxvi-xxxix. As we have already seen, this section of literature about the prophets has been used by the compiler of II Kings, though there are differences between the two selections.

One interesting feature of the book is the amount of oracular prose. As a rule this appears in cases where the prophet has recorded his own utterances, in other words in the second class of material used by the compilers. There are usually signs which suggest that the oracle was originally given in poetic form, and has been " prosified " in course of transmission. This may have happened in other books, but here the prose and poetry slide into one another as they seldom do elsewhere.

We may distinguish the following smaller collections in the Book of Isaiah :

(i) Ch. i. A series of short oracles, probably five in number, though the lines of demarcation are not so clear towards the end as they are at the beginning.

(ii) Chs. ii-iv, with ch. v attached. The section consists mainly of denunciations uttered against the sins of Israel and Judah, with varied threats of punishment. It includes two prose passages; the first of these, iii, 18-23, is a sort of milliner's catalogue inserted into a denunciation of the women, and may well be a later addition to the original oracle. Ch. iv, 3-6 is a promise of a better time when the nation has been purified. Here, again, we may suspect a later addition to the original collection, whether it is due to Isaiah or to another, for collectors and compilers liked to finish their work with a happy, or at least hopeful, passage. Ch. v begins with the prophet's adaptation of a popular song (or so we may conjecture), and the special application of it to the people of Judah. The rest of the chapter is a collection of " Woes," threats of punishment for certain specific types of sinners. It finishes with an account of what Yahweh will be like and of what He will do when He appears in His might. Two other " Woes " appear in ch. x, and some scholars think they have been accidentally transferred from this chapter. More probably they came into the hands only of another collector. The second of the two (x, 5ff.) refers to Assyria, not to Israel at all.

(iii) Chs. vi-xii. At the head of this collection stands the great story of Isaiah's call. Other prose passages are introduced, either by the individual collector, or by the compiler, who wished to include other material which came from the same general period as most of his oracular pieces. The greatest number of the sections here seem to come from the years when Pekah and Rezin were trying to force Judah into an alliance against Assyria (see p. 70). We have a prose oracle in x, 24-27, and the beautiful Messianic picture in ch. xi almost certainly comes from a time not earlier than the exile. The term rendered " stock " (R.V.; A.V. " stem ") really means the stump left in the ground after a tree has been cut down. It could hardly have been used in this connection while the house of David was still on the throne. Ch. xii consists of two little Psalms. Once more we see how the collector liked to have a happy ending to his collection.

(iv) Chs. xiii-xxiii. This is, apparently, a collection of oracles directed against foreign nations. Collectors were fond of accumulating material of this kind; one whole book (Obadiah) is of this class, and, apart from the opening Psalm, Nahum is entirely concerned with the fall of Nineveh. In this kind of collection, more than in any other, we are likely to find oracles which do not belong to the prophet with whose utterances they are included. In several instances these " foreign " oracles have been included in the books of more than one prophet. Here they are normally introduced with the word " Massa," which properly means " burden," but can be used of an oracle.

The first nation dealt with in the Isaiah collection is Babylon (chs. xiii, xiv). Now Babylon was hardly an oppressor of Israel in Isaiah's day, as the great taunt-song in ch. xiv would suggest, and many scholars believe that these two chapters come from the period of the exile.

To the Babylon section two short oracles are appended, one dealing with Assyria (xiv, 24-27), and one with Philistia (xiv, 28-32). The latter is dated in the year in which Ahaz died, and may be a warning to the Philistines that Sargon will prove more dangerous than any of his predecessors.

Chs. xv, xvi deal with Moab. Several of the pieces are found also in the "foreign" collection of the Book of Jeremiah (Jer. xlviii) and may be the work of an otherwise unknown prophet.

Ch. xvii contains five pieces. The first definitely attacks Damascus (xvii, 1-3), but the other four (xvii, 4-6, 7-8, 9-11, 12-14) are more general, and no enemy is named.

Ethiopia, i.e. southern Egypt, is the subject of ch. xviii. The oracle contained in this chapter is connected with an embassy sent to Judah, and the occasion may well have been the general revolt against Sennacherib, provoked by Babylon and Egypt.

The "Massa" of Egypt is contained in ch. xix. There is a long poetic oracle in vv. 1-15, followed by a series of short utterances in prose form. The last of these, vv. 23-25, seems to predict a time when there shall be general peace between the three great world-powers, Egypt, Assyria, and Israel. In ch. xx we return to Egypt, and Isaiah is bidden go barefoot and lightly clad to indicate the coming slavery of Egypt.

Ch. xxi, 1-10 is something of a mystery. It is headed "The Massa of the Wilderness of the Sea (or West)." Some scholars think that the text is at fault here, for the west is not a wilderness region from the Palestinian point of view; on the contrary the coastal plain is one of the most fertile districts in the land. Two pieces are included, vv. 1-5 describe the prophet's experience and terror at the approach of some calamity. In vv. 6-10 we have an account of the way in which a prophet prepared himself to receive the divine word, and of that which actually came to him, foretelling the destruction of Babylon. The mention of Babylon has led a number of scholars to think that this oracle was the work of a prophet who lived in Mesopotamia during the exile.

Edom appears to be the subject of the short oracle in xxi, 11-15; there is evidence to suggest that the name "Dumah" is a copyist's mistake for Edom. The last two verses of the chapter predict calamity for the Bedouin tribe of Kedar. It is to be noted that all through the chapter the prophet speaks in the first person, though all except the last two verses is in poetic form.

Ch. xxii does not appear to deal with a foreign nation, but with Judah itself. The title is " Massa of the Valley of Vision," and the reference is clearly to some actual event in Jerusalem. The whole section, vv. 1-14 may be a single oracle, though this is unusually long, and there may be divisions at the end of vv. 4 and 11. The rest of the chapter describes what we should call in modern terms a change of ministry. A scribe named Shebna, one of the chief officials in the kingdom, is to be dismissed from office, and his place is to be taken by a man named Eliakim. There seems no good reason for doubting that all the pieces in the chapter come from Isaiah himself, though the mention of Elam in v. 6 is difficult to explain unless it is taken as an abnormal alternative for Assyria.

In the " Massa " against Tyre (ch. xxiii) we have first three oracles, of which the two last especially mention Tarshish, vv. 1-5, 6-9, and 10-14. These are followed by a couple of prose oracles (vv. 15-16 and 17-18), one of which introduces a poetic couplet in v. 16.

With the section xxiv-xxvii we are in a totally different atmosphere from that we have found up to this point. We are no longer reading prophecy of the ordinary type, but a special sort of literature which embodies conceptions of the way in which the established order will end—" Eschatology." Writings of this kind are called " Apocalyptic "; " Apocalypse " is the Greek word for " Revelation." Here we have an early form of Apocalypse, though it is possibly later than the time of Isaiah. It offers a great picture of a triumphal feast in honour of Yahweh, who has overthrown all enemies and inaugurated His own reign. From time to time songs of victory and praise are inserted, which tend to heighten the general sense of exultation. In xxv, 8 we have one of the very rare indications—rare in the Old Testament—of belief in eternal life. Here, however, it is not a question of resurrection after death, or a new life in another world, but the abolition of death altogether. Israel made more than one tentative effort at grasping the future life before it developed that clear doctrine which we find among the Pharisees in New Testament times.

The fifth of the collections is to be found in xxviii-xxxv. Here we are taken back to Israel once more. The first oracle, xxviii, 1-4, is a threat against Samaria, and must be earlier than 724 B.C. This is followed by a kind of eschatological appendix in vv. 5-6. Vv. 7-8 describe the foul effects of a revel, and vv. 9-13 speak of the mockery to which the prophet was exposed. The oracle is of special interest, because it suggests what may have happened when a prophet fell under the influence of his special condition. It seems that he did not describe his experience till it had passed; the only sounds he uttered while it lasted formed a series of unintelligible noises. The words rendered " line " and " precept " in vv. 10 and 13 are really meaningless sounds, " baby talk," and that is all the observer will get unless he listens to the word which has been given to the prophet to repeat to the people at a later stage.

These last oracles may be addressed either to Samaria or to Jerusalem, but in vv.14-15 we are certainly in the south, confronted with that necromancy which Isaiah denounced elsewhere (viii, 19-22). To this the compiler has attached vv. 16-22, in which the contrast is drawn between this false cult and the benefits which accrue from the true worship of Yahweh. Vv. 23-29 illustrate Yahweh's different modes of dealing with men, compared to the varying methods of the farmer.

Ch. xxix opens with an oracle which refers, as it seems, to danger threatening Jerusalem, probably from some enemy. The whole piece runs from v. 1 to v. 8, but some scholars feel that the reversal of fortune suggested in vv. 7-8 is a later addition to the original form. In that case it was probably appended before the piece was taken over by the collector. Vv. 9-12 depict the people as staggering blindly in the wrath of Yahweh; the last two verses are a prose commentary on the first two. Vv. 13-14 condemn the hypocrisy of superficial worship. Vv. 15-21 may be a single utterance, but the two opening verses are somewhat obscure, and their tone is not carried through to the end of v. 21. The contrast between the humble and the lofty is characteristic of later writings, though this in itself is not enough to make Isaiah's authorship impossible. In vv. 22-24 were apparently placed where they are in order to give the section a happy ending.

Chs. xxx, xxxi possibly formed an independent small collection. They are concerned chiefly with Egypt, and we may ask why they were included with ch. xix. The reason may be that they have specific reference to the danger of alliance with Egypt, and the disasters which will fall upon that country are simply incidental. There is an interesting note in xxx, 8, where the prophet is ordered to write down the oracle he has just uttered. This is the first definite indication of a prophet taking such a course, and here it applies only to a single oracle. The last two sections of ch. xxx (19-26 and 27-33) are a promise of the blessings which will follow on obedience to the word of Yahweh; the first is in prose, and the second in verse form. Ch. xxxi contains three oracles. The first (vv. 1-3) repeats the warning against contamination with Egypt, the second (vv. 4-5, with a prose addition in vv. 6-7) announces the divine protection of Jerusalem, and the third (vv. 8-9) amplifies the last by predicting the miraculous defeat of Assyria.

Ch. xxxii begins with a Messianic passage, in which an ideal king is promised to Israel (vv. 1-8). The effects of his government include a righting of men's false perspective. Vv. 9-20 give the impression of two pieces telescoped into one. The opening verses (9-12) are a prose denunciation of the women, but they merge into a description of a good time coming, in which traces of poetry are seen. It is possible that in vv. 15-20 we have another separate oracle, which has been mutilated at the beginning.

The first verse of ch. xxxiii seems to be independent of the rest, and may be the beginning of a poem of which the remainder has not been preserved. It serves here as an introduction to the three pieces which the chapter contains, vv. 2-6, 7-12, 13-24. These depict the distress of Jerusalem and look forward to a coming deliverance and the triumph of Yahweh. Many scholars feel that they came from a later period than that of Isaiah, though it is possible to refer them to events which took place in his lifetime.

Ch. xxxiv, too, is usually held to be exilic or post-exilic. It is a kind of " Apocalypse," in which the victory of Yahweh over His enemies is described in rather brutal terms. It seems to have been a single continuous poem, though it may include elements drawn from other sources.

Ch. xxxv gives us one of the most beautiful pictures of restoration which our Bible contains. The ransomed of Yahweh are to return from their exile to their old home. All nature is transformed, and a great causeway rises across the desert for the safe transport of the redeemed. Clearly the situation indicated is that of captive Judah after the exile, possibly immediately on the accession of Cyrus, or possibly at the time of some later migration, such as that which took place in the days of Ezra.

This collection of oracular material is followed by a prose section chs. xxxvi-xxxix. As we have already seen, these narratives were taken from a collection of stories about Isaiah, which was also used by the compiler of II Kings. The two records are not identical; in the prophetic book we have no mention of Hezekiah's submission to Sennacherib (II Kings xviii, 14-16), and the historian omits the song of thanksgiving ascribed to Hezekiah in Is. xxxviii, 9-20. The two authors may have had different forms of the record before them, or they may have made a deliberate selection from a common document.

We have thus all the familiar features of a normal prophetic book. All three types of material are used, and the basis of the work is a series of collections embodying the utterances of the prophet. Some of the individual collections, and also the book as a whole (up to this point) seem to have been expanded by the addition of prophecy which comes from some other than Isaiah. There is, too, the tendency to finish a collection on a happy note, leading at the end to the magnificent outburst of ch. xxxv.

While Isaiah shares with other pre-exilic prophets the doctrines which have already been indicated (pp. 79-81), he has his own special point of view. This is conditioned by the circumstances of his original call to the prophetic ministry, as described in ch. vi. What has impressed him more than anything else is the holiness, the sanctity, of Yahweh. Several explanations of the terms have been given. It has been traced back to that sense of awe, and even of terror, which may be inspired by the unknown elements in life, the mysterious and inexplicable features of experience in the world about him. It has thus been connected with the common primitive belief in the *tabu*, the thing that may not be touched with impunity because it carries with it a hidden power belonging to some spirit or to some yet more uncertain and vague influence, a mystery which makes men shudder with fear. The " holy " thing or person must be isolated—perhaps we might almost say " insulated," for the influence may be conveyed by physical contact. There are experts who know how the holy person may be approached in safety, and their directions must be accurately carried out. So arises the idea of separation from common life, and of reservation for purposes of religion.

But Isaiah went further. To him the holiness of Yahweh had a moral content. No other religion of the ancient world so strongly emphasised the moral character and demands of a deity as did that faith which Israel owed to Moses. It was on this element that all the great prophets of the eighth and seventh centuries fastened, but it was especially Isaiah who saw in it an essential part of Yahweh's holiness. It had a double aspect. In the first place it meant that Yahweh was in a sense consecrated to Israel; they were His people in a peculiar sense; He had chosen them and would do for them what he would do for no other nation.

But there was another side. Israel must be holy to Yahweh. Most pious Israelites would have agreed, but Isaiah carried the doctrine into all departments of life. He has been represented as a keen-eyed statesman, who knew that his country would be ignored by the great world-powers, and therefore insisted that she must pursue a policy of isolation. But his true reason seems to have been fear that contact with other nations would lead to spiritual contamination with other gods —a fear justified by the religious policy imposed on Judah by Assyria.

The Book of Isaiah goes beyond ch. xxxix. The remaining twenty-seven chapters are practically all in poetic form. As soon as we read the opening verse of ch. xl we find ourselves in a totally new atmosphere. Yahweh is coming back to Jerusalem, and His return is to inaugurate a new life for His people. The kings of the house of David have disappeared, the only contemporary king mentioned by name is Cyrus, who conquered Babylon in 538 B.C., two centuries after the time of Isaiah. The whole background of these chapters is that of Israel in exile, looking for immediate deliverance and restoration. Babylon, not Assyria, is the great world power, and the overthrow of that great city is expected in the near future. The name of Isaiah never occurs after the end of ch. xxxix. All these considerations, and others connected with the style and outlook of the new section, have led most modern scholars to the belief that here we have a collection of prophecies uttered by a man whose very name is unknown to us, but who lived in Babylon (one or two would place him in Syria or elsewhere in the west) when the victories of Cyrus, king of Persia, were beginning to threaten the Babylonian empire. It is, of course, not impossible that Isaiah was transported into a period two hundred years later than his own time, but nowhere else have we anything like a parallel, and it is more natural to suppose that the work of one of our greatest prophets was collected and preserved as a single whole, being placed after the Book of Isaiah (i.e. Is. i-xxxix). As it had no name at its head, it would readily be copied as a continuous document with the original book of Isaiah. The position of these chapters may well be due to certain links with the prophet of Is. i-xxxix, e.g. the common use of the epithet " Holy One of Israel " applied to Yahweh. But, whoever may have been the author, or by whatever means these chapters reached their present position, they can be rightly interpreted and applied only when we see them in the light of events which occurred between 548 and 538 B.C.

During the last fifty years, however, there has grown up a strong feeling that in Is. xl-lxvi we have not one collection but two. When we come to ch. lvi we are conscious of another change in atmosphere. The people seem to be back in their own land, and the points on which stress is laid are not exactly the same as those most prominent in xl-lv. There is a certain interest in ritual, and Babylon is never mentioned by name.

As we read through chs. xl-lv there are certain themes which come to the front again and again. The opening words : " Comfort ye, comfort ye," might serve, in a sense, as a motto for the whole. Yahweh is coming back to His own city and sanctuary and His people may follow. They are constantly in need of encouragement; they are a poor, neglected and oppressed nation, small in numbers and without influence. But they are still the people of Yahweh, the God of the whole earth. For the first time in the history of Israel a clear and unmistakable challenge of Monotheism rings out. Earlier prophets had insisted that Yahweh was the only God to be worshipped by Israel, but they had seldom denied the existence of others. Even our Psalms at times use language which imply that others exist, though they are inferior to Yahweh. But here we have statements addressed to the gods of Babylon, such as " You are less than nothing " (xli, 24). Nebo, Marduk, and the rest, are no more than minus quantities.

Israel has been through a time of terrible affliction, but there has been a reason for it. Even the opening message of comfort stresses the fact that her sufferings are due to her sins, and these have meant the pain, even the enslavement, of Yahweh Himself (xliii, 22-24). But so great is His love for them that He has been ready to go to any lengths to restore them, and one of the regular epithets He applies to Himself is " thy Redeemer."

Included in the work of this prophet is a series of passages which draw a picture of an ideal servant of Yahweh. They are xlii, 1-4, xlix, 1-6, 1, 4-9, and lii, 13-liii, 12. In the first it is Yahweh who speaks, in the second and the third it is the servant himself, and the last is put into the mouth of observers who have misunderstood him during his life, but after his shameful death have grasped the meaning of his work and of his sacrifice. Many attempts have been made to discover a historical character who sat unconsciously for this portrait. Various individuals have been suggested—Jeremiah, Zerubbabel, the nameless prophet himself, or even Moses. Others, recognising the Israelite view of " corporate personality," have held that the Servant was either Israel as a whole or a select minority within the nation. The Christian Church has normally held that we have here a prediction of the life and sufferings of Christ, a view which is sound in principle, though it must not be pressed too far in detail. The ideal Servant, for example, is depicted in Is. liii as a leper. The safest line of exegesis is to recognise that we have here a picture of an ideal Servant of God, and that any person who willingly undertakes that service may have to face similar experience. Since Jesus is the only perfect Servant of God whom the world has ever seen, it will be in Him that the prophecy finds its most complete fulfilment. Apart from Ps. xxiii, there is no passage in the Old Testament which is better known or means more to the Christian spirit than this does.

Chs. lvi-lxvi are much more varied than the preceding sixteen. There are exhortations to keep the law, to admit into the community people who might otherwise be left outside, and to avoid false worship. Some passages recall the great prophet of the exile (especially lxi). Others denounce the sins of the people, not as past iniquities for which punishment is now inflicted, but as current evils in the national life. There are passages which tell us of a magnificent future for Israel, such as ch. lx, where we have one of the finest poems in the Old Testament. The whole is clearly a collection (perhaps there was originally more than one) of rather miscellaneous oracles coming, possibly, from different prophets and different times, but bearing sufficient resemblance to the rest of the book to explain its attachment to Is. xl-lv.

CHAPTER XII

THE LATER PROPHETS: JEREMIAH

THE life of Jeremiah falls in one of those periods of transition when the whole aspect of the political world changes in a single generation. When he was born, the greatest of the world-powers was Assyria. Egypt, though only in the second rank, was still a force with which men had to reckon, and might once more assert her ancient claims to dominance. Babylon was a subject state within the Assyrian empire, though she was always a thorn in the side of her mistress. There were other tribes to the east and north, but they offered little more than a vague threat, and the chief danger to be feared from them was a series of more or less effective raids. Judah was still a nominally independent kingdom, though paying tribute to Assyria.

When Jeremiah died, Assyria had been wiped off the map of the world. Egypt had made her last bid for the hegemony of civilisation. Judah had ceased to exist as a political entity; Jerusalem and its Temple were a heap of blackened ruins. Babylon was supreme, and for three quarters of a century her lordship remained unchallenged by any people in the world.

Even before the final catastrophe, great changes had taken place in Judah itself. The great invasion from the north which broke up the northern defences of the Assyrian empire, also ravaged Judah, and even threatened Jerusalem, though without effect. Five years later, in 621 B.C., a book of the Law was discovered in the Temple, and on its basis a complete religious revolution was carried out in Judah and extended further north, for the collapse of the Assyrian power had left this distant province unprotected. The tragic death of Josiah left Judah at the mercy, first of Egypt and then of Babylon.

Egyptian intrigues induced one king after another to revolt against Babylon, and at length the final blow fell. With the murder of Gedaliah, the last remnant of organised authority in Judah failed, and Jeremiah himself was taken with other fugitives to Egypt. It is against this background of events that we must see the life and work of this prophet.

In general structure the Book of Jeremiah may be compared with Isaiah i-xxxix. It contains material of all three types, but there is more of the autobiographical prose here than in any other book except that of Ezekiel, and more of the biographical prose than in any other prophetic book. The prophetic oracles came into the final compiler's hands as a series of separate collections, and were used by him as the basis of his construction, so far as was possible. There was a considerable mass of material dealing with foreign nations which was kept quite separate from all the rest.

It is possible that we owe to Jeremiah's " secretary," the scribe Baruch, most of the prose in the book, perhaps nearly all. The sections in the first person (autobiographical prose) may well have been taken from the roll which Baruch wrote at Jeremiah's dictation (Jer. xxxvi). The detailed narratives of the prophet's life and experiences were clearly the work of a contemporary, and none was in a better position to write them than the man who was so closely connected with the prophet (cf. xliii, 3). It is interesting to find that at least one event was noted in both forms of prose; the actual message of the prophet is given to us in vii, 1-20, while the circumstances which accompanied its delivery are described in xxvi.

The compiler's method is fairly obvious. He took a small collection of poetic oracles, and placed at its head a section from the autobiographical prose, arranging the material roughly in chronological order. When he had exhausted, or nearly exhausted the available stock of this type, he prefixed to his collection a piece of the biographical prose. A considerable amount of this material was still left over, and he placed this at the end.

This was his general plan, but there were variations from it. In ch. xiv, for example, a prose section is inserted in the middle of a poetic collection. In ch. xvii we have such a passage at the end of the poetic oracles. Ch. xxii contains a series of utterances dealing with the kings of Judah whom Jeremiah had known; it may have formed a single collection, and it is to be noted that there is no piece devoted to Josiah, whom the prophet respected and admired. Ch. xxv contains all three types, biographical prose being followed by an auto-biographical section before the short oracular poetry is intro-duced. Chs. xxx-xxxiii form a group by themselves, which has been called " The Book of the Future of Judah." Here the poetic section stands first, followed by the prose. And, finally, in the Hebrew Bible, the collection of oracles against foreign nations is placed right at the end of the book, with only a purely historical chapter after it, taken largely from the same source as the closing chapter of II Kings. It is to be remarked, however, that the Egyptian Jews had a form of the book in which the foreign oracles were placed after xxv, 13, v. 14 being omitted, and xxv, 15ff coming at the end of this whole collection. The result is that in the Greek version the chapter and verse references are all quite different from those in our Bible, till we come to ch. lii. We do not know why this difference exists. It is possible that the earliest form of the book did not contain this collection at all, and that different communities of Jews inserted it in different places. Or one of the two may have felt that another place was more suitable; in that case it may well be that the Egyptian order was original.

The first collection extends down to iii, 5. It is introduced by the story of Jeremiah's call, and the introduction merges into the poetic oracle at i, 15. The utterances contained in this collection may all have come from the earliest period of Jeremiah's work, from 626 to 621 B.C., and seem to be strongly influenced by Hosea.

Ch. iii, 6-18 are in prose (1st person) and are followed by the second main collection, which extends from iii, 19 to vi, 30. Most of these oracles, too, are earlier than the pro-mulgation of the Deuteronomic law, and some may refer to the invasion of the northern hordes in 626, the year of Jeremiah's call.

To the third collection is prefixed the prose passage vii, 1-viii, 3, which might well have been a summary of what Jeremiah had to say as an advocate of the Deuteronomic reform. On the other hand the second piece (viii, 8-9) in the collection which follows suggests that the prophet had been disillusioned as to the value of the reform. The second line in v. 8 may be read in two ways, either " The lying pen of the scribes has wrought falsely," which suggests that Jeremiah had discovered the whole to be a forgery, or " The lying pen of the scribes has made it into a lie," which rather implies that the original form had suffered from tampering by the scribes. There is a widespread feeling that in ch. x we have utterances from a later prophet(s); v. 11 is not Hebrew, but Aramaic.

In ch. xi we have Jeremiah's first introduction to the newly-found Law. He seems to have accepted it with some enthusiasm, and to have accepted a commission as one of the agents whose duty it was to proclaim the law among the people. The poetic collection which follows (xi, 15-xii, 13) gives us something which is unusual outside Jeremiah, a poetic account of the prophet's own experience, his doubts and his attempts at rebellion against the burden of prophecy, together with the hostility of those about him. No other prophet has allowed us to see so much of his inner struggles, and such passages are not the least valuable and impressive of Jeremiah's utterances. Here, in xii 1-5 he propounds the problem of suffering, or rather, of the unfair incidence of suffering, and is warned that worse is in store for him. We shall meet this question again when we come to the work of Habakkuk. At the end the collector, or perhaps the compiler, has appended a prose passage which holds out a hope of prosperity if only the people will resume their allegiance to Yahweh.

Ch. xiii, 1-14 describe one of those symbolic actions which are characteristic of many prophets. It is important to remember that these were regarded as a kind of sympathetic magic, an action done on a small scale which produced a much larger event—like whistling for a wind. The prophet's actions, as well as his words, might well be productive for the future. The small collection which follows may have been assigned by the collector to the reign of Jehoiachin. The mention of the queen-mother in v. 18 suggests that she had considerable influence, which is more likely to have happened with a very young man than with an older king.

Ch. xiv opens with an oracle concerning a drought, in which we note the prophet's sympathy for the wild animals (v. 5). Then comes the prose introduction, followed by a poetic collection which carries us down to xv, 21. There are signs of modification, in some verses, e.g. xv, 3-4 appear in

Jeremiah's characteristic prose style. In xv, 15-21 we have another of those personal self-revelations which we have already met in ch. xii. It takes the form of a conversation between Jeremiah and Yahweh, and at the end the prophet is told that he may be restored to his office if he will cease thinking about his own troubles.

Ch. xvi opens with a direct command to Jeremiah not to marry and raise a family. The reason is that fearful calamity is to fall on Judah because of her sin. In vv. 14-15 a compiler has lightened the burden by introducing a message of hope from xxiii, 7-8, and the first poetic passage is a little Psalm of trust and the assurance that the people will some day come to the true faith. The short collection of poetic oracles extends from xvii, 1-18, but it includes unusual material, e.g. a Psalm in vv. 7-8, which looks like the basis of the first piece in our Psalter. To this collection has been appended a warning against desecration of the Sabbath (xvii, 19-27).

The next collection, xviii, 13-23, is again very short; it is introduced by the story of Jeremiah's visit to the potter, and it closes with another of the prophet's prayers (vv. 19-23).

xix, 1-xx, 6 forms the first piece taken from the biographical collection used by the compiler. It describes a clash between Jeremiah and a Temple official, who put the prophet in the stocks for a night. The passage introduces the most terrible utterance we have from any writer of the Old Testament. Even Jeremiah had not fully grasped the true character of God, and still held to the common belief that He could and did use the prophetic inspiration to " seduce " men to their ruin. There is a technical term which, in this peculiar sense, occurs only in three Biblical passages. In I Kings xxii Ahab is " seduced " to destruction by the lying spirit in the mouth of his prophets, and in Ez. xiv, 9 we have the direct statement that the prophet himself might be " seduced " by divine inspiration. The test of true inspiration was the fulfilment of his word, and for long years Jeremiah had foretold the ruin of Jerusalem. So he and those about him felt that he was a " seduced " prophet, and he was exposed both to the mockery of the people, and to the inner conflict between the divine power and the human reluctance.

Ch. xxi contains a short oracle directed to the king (vv. 12-14), to which is prefixed a biographical passage dated in the reign of Zedekiah, and, more particularly during the final siege of Jerusalem. Ch. xxii is a small collection by itself, devoted to the kings. It is a curious mixture of poetry and prose; the collector or compiler has drawn on both sources. At the head stands a general exhortation to just government, followed by a poetic oracle of doom (vv. 1-5, 6-7), a pair of prose verses describing the gathering of nations against Jerusalem. The first king mentioned is Jehoahaz, here named Shallum. This was probably his personal name, the other being adopted as a " throne-name " on his accession. The little oracle has a special interest, since it occurs in two forms. V. 10 gives it in the original verse, and vv. 11-12 in prose, showing how a poetic utterance might be expanded when reduced to prose. The oracle on Jehoiakim (vv. 13-19) is a bitter denunciation of the bold, bad king, who neither feared God nor regarded man, and this is followed by an address to an unnamed feminine individual, probably Jerusalem personified (vv. 20-23). The rest of the chapter is given to Jehoiachin (here named Coniah—the same name with the two elements inverted). It consists of a series of short prose utterances, and it is interesting to note that special mention is made of the queen-mother (v. 26).

This group dealing with the kings may be continued in xxiii, 1-8. It opens with a prose section, promising restoration under a king whose name is given in the following short poetic oracle (vv. 5-6) as " Yahweh-sidquenu." It has been suggested that this is intended to be an inversion of " Zedekiah," to whom there is no other reference in this section.

Another specialised collection follows, this time dealing with the popular prophets (xxiii, 9-40). Here the poetic oracles precede the prose sections, and again we may suspect that this arrangement is due to a collector rather than to a compiler.

Ch. xxiv is a prose passage in the first person, and describes the lesson Jeremiah learned from contemplating two baskets of figs. This incident is to be placed soon after the deportation of Jehoiachin, for the old leaders of the people are compared to good figs, while their successors are like figs so rotten that it made the beholder sick to look at them. Parables of this kind, drawn from actual objects before the prophet's eyes, are characteristic of Jeremiah, *cf*. i, 11-12, 13-14, xviii, 1-12.

Ch. xxv is concerned with foreign nations, and its peculiar structure has already been noted. As already suggested (p. 94) the collection in chs. xlvi-li would fit the place it is given in the Egyptian tradition, i.e. where xxv, 15 stands in the Hebrew text and the English versions.

Ch. xxvi gives us the circumstances attending Jeremiah's utterance of the prophecies contained in vii, 1-20. It has one point of great interest. In defending Jeremiah against the ecclesiastical authorities the elders of the people quote verbatim Mi. iii, 12, giving the name of the prophet to whom they appeal. In no other case does a prophetic book give us this kind of direct evidence to the wording and authorship of a passage found in another prophetic book.

No doubt Jeremiah's contemporaries would have called him a " collaborationist " if they had known the word. He certainly urged submission to Nebuchadnezzar, and in ch. xxvii he is said to have sent a message to the tribes bordering on Judah, urging them to accept Babylonian rule (xxvii, 1-11). The passage is followed by a similar exhortation to Zedekiah, warning him that he must remain faithful to his overlord, and in both cases denouncing the prophets who advised revolt against the Mesopotamian power. The spelling of the Babylonian king's name is interesting. It occurs between thirty and forty times in this book, and in the great majority of these places is correctly spelled Nebuchadrezzar. In the section xxvii, xxviii, however, the better-known but inaccurate spelling Nebuchadnezzar is found, and this appears also in the opening verses of ch. xxix. It is difficult to explain this except as a peculiarity of some scribe who copied these chapters and these alone in an early MS which was followed by all that came after it.

Ch. xxviii belongs to the biographical type; the appearance of the first person in v. 1 is probably due to a copyist's error. It is an extremely interesting passage, throwing light on the nature of prophecy in the last years of the monarchy. Jeremiah performs a symbolic action, making a yoke to typify the subjection of the west to Nebuchadnezzar. Another prophet, of the popular and " patriotic " type, also performs a symbolic action; he breaks the yoke which Jeremiah has made, and predicts that his deed will produce its results within two years. To the eye of the public, the two men are of the same class. They use the same language, and claim to have had the same kind of experience. Even Jeremiah admits that Hananiah's claim is just, and hopes that his word may be fulfilled. At the same time, he insists that while a word spoken by a prophet of doom may remain unfulfilled, yet a prediction of prosperity can be the true word of Yahweh only if it comes to pass. But Jeremiah is instructed also to further action, and to make an iron yoke which Hananiah cannot break. This new revelation has made it clear that Hananiah's claims to inspiration are false, and that he is misleading the people; he will die within two years if Jeremiah is right. The event justifies Jeremiah, and Hananiah dies.

Among the exiles taken to Babylon with Jehoiachin were a number of prophets. One of them we know well, Ezekiel. He was a disciple of Jeremiah, but there were others (names are given in xxix, 21) who took the same view as Hananiah had done. Accordingly Jeremiah sent a letter to the exiles in general, warning them that they would do well to accept their new position and become good citizens of Babylon, for seventy years (xxix, 10) would pass before they were restored to their own land. The letter is given in xxix, 4-23. In xxix, 24-32 we have a more personal matter. An exiled prophet has written to the priests in Jerusalem, demanding the arrest and punishment of Jeremiah. It is the business of the priest to keep these " ecstatics " out of the Temple, and Zephaniah has failed in his duty. For this Jeremiah predicts that the offender shall have no part in any benefit which Jeremiah may foretell.

With ch. xxx begins a new section of the book. It opens with a collection of poetic oracles. They are very mixed; some are in the old style, and predict disaster. Of these the best-known is, perhaps, xxxi, 15, where Rachel in her tomb mourns the desolation of Benjamin. On the other hand we have in xxxi, 2-6 one of the loveliest oracles in the Old Testament, and there is real exultation in such a piece as xxxi, 7-9. Ch. xxxi, 23-40 is mainly a prose collection, with occasional snatches of verse, such as the popular saying in v. 29, used by Ezekiel as the text for the address we find in Ez. xviii. It lays down the principle of individualism in religion as against the theory that men suffer disaster as punishment for the sins of earlier generations. Here, too, we find the great prediction of the new covenant (xxxi, 31-34), which marks a stage in human knowledge of God.

Ch. xxxii exhibits Jeremiah as the great optimist. It begins with his purchase of ancestral land, and with the care he took to preserve the title deeds. The city was besieged, and Jeremiah himself was convinced of its ruin, yet he knew also that restoration would come.

Ch. xxxiii continues in the same strain; there will be terrible punishment, but that will not be the end. Vv. 14-26 were not included in the Egyptian text, and may have been a later addition to this section.

Ch. xxxiv records utterances of Jeremiah during the last siege of Jerusalem. Vv. 1-7 are addressed to Zedekiah, and foretell the fate which will befall him. The rest of the chapter condemns certain people for a grave social wrong. Israelite law ordained that a slave should not be kept against his will in his master's service for more than six years. This had been disregarded, till the threat to Jerusalem had made the owners come back to their duty. The siege was raised for a time, and the owners took back their slaves. The offence was aggravated by the fact that these men had entered into a solemn covenant (v. 18), undertaking to observe this law. So their punishment was certain.

Ch. xxxv is the last of the autobiographical passages in the book. It goes back to the reign of Jehoiakim, and describes a symbolic action of a kind. Jeremiah takes certain Rechabites and invites them to drink wine. They refuse, and their fidelity to their rules is held up before the rest of the people in condemnation of the latter.

Ch. xxxvi tells the dramatic story of the roll prepared by Baruch at Jeremiah's dictation. The date is 605/4, i.e. soon after the battle of Carchemish, which finally wrecked the hopes of Egypt. As yet Judah is in no immediate danger, but the Babylonian advance cannot be long delayed.

With ch. xxxvii we enter on the last years of the monarchy. The story is practically continuous, and gives a vivid picture of Jerusalem during the final siege, and of the experiences through which Jeremiah passed. As a " defeatist " he was unpopular, and suffered imprisonment. Zedekiah himself was not unfriendly, but lacked the moral force to withstand the more violent of his nobles. Once the prophet was lowered into a well which was empty except for deep mud at the bottom. He was left to starve, but was rescued by a negro slave named Ebedmelech (xxxviii, 4-13). After the fall of the city he was well treated by the Chaldeans, and was allowed to stay with Gedaliah. When the latter was murdered Jeremiah protested against the flight into Egypt, but was carried there against his will, to continue his prophetic work in exile. Others fell into the ways of the people about them, especially in worshipping the Queen of Heaven (probably Isis, whom they may have identified with the Canaanite goddess Anath). Jeremiah had to tell them that this meant the end of their association with Yahweh. They had broken the Covenant for the last time; He would no more be their God nor they His people. It was indeed the end for Jeremiah, and death could not be a worse fate. But even then he could hear Yahweh saying: " They shall know whose word shall stand, mine or theirs."

Ch. xlv is a private message given to Baruch. He, the prophet's secretary, sharing Jeremiah's troubles without his inspiration, asked what his reward would be, and the answer was simply that his life would be saved in the midst of the universal destruction. So he survived, and, in the land of exile, compiled for us his narratives of the greatest among the goodly fellowship of the prophets.

The collection of foreign oracles occupies chs. xlvi-li. Some scholars have held that no part of them is to be ascribed to Jeremiah, but if there is any value in the test of style, large portions of them cannot be denied to him. Probably there are later additions, but we suspect them especially at the end of each group. Thus the first people to be attacked are the Egyptians (xlvi), and in the last verses of the chapter we may well have an exilic piece (vv. 27-28). Ch. xlvii deals with the Philistines, and ch. xlviii with Moab. This includes a prose passage (vv. 34-40), and several pieces which appear also in the Isaiah collection relating to Moab. The subject of xlix, 1-6 is Ammon, followed by Edom (vv. 7-22; some oracles were used by the compiler of Obadiah), Damascus (vv. 23-27), Kedar and Hazor (vv. 28-33) and Elam (vv. 34-39). Chs. l and li deal with Babylon, and the whole of these two chapters is probably to be ascribed to the same period as Isaiah xl-lv. In this section we have a certain amount of oracle in prose form, and there is one oracle (l, 41-43) which was originally applied to Judah, and is found in Jer. vi, 22-24. It has been adapted to Babylon by a simple change of name, and it seems to have come into the hands of this collector in a multilated form, for the last lines in ch. vi are missing here.

The compiler has rounded off his book with an extract from the annals of Judah, giving a few details which have not been preserved in II Kings. The original source, however, seems to have been the same in both cases. Jeremiah is not mentioned in this narrative, which ends with the release of Jehoiachin.

Jeremiah's contribution to our spiritual thinking is made in two directions. He added little to the actual teaching of his great eighth-century predecessors, but he has allowed us to see his inner life as not even Hosea has done. In its earlier stages religion is a matter for the whole community; the individual is either a representative or a member of that community. Thus, when David is speaking of the treatment accorded to him by his enemies, he says " They have driven me out . . . saying, Go, worship other gods " (I Sam. xxvi, 19). But the effect of Jeremiah's struggles against the divine commission was to isolate him and set him alone with his God. His relation to Yahweh was essentially personal rather than national; when they spoke together the nation and the world were shut out. It is not surprising that Jeremiah so emphatically proclaimed that individualism which was later to be developed by Ezekiel. From this intimate and personal contact with God Jeremiah was the first of all those who in Israel and after Israel have known the experience of communion with God in a world where all else was excluded. He was, as has been said, the father of all the saints.

If we would understand the second point, an even more striking contribution to Christian thought, we must follow the story of his attitude to the Covenant. On the discovery of Deuteronomy he had accepted it wholeheartedly, and become one of its missionaries among his own people (cf. ch. xi.). Disillusionment came, and he realised that no mere book could do what was needed (cf. viii, 8). So at last he reached the truth that there must be a new covenant. Its terms would be the same as those of the old covenant; the novelty would be in the way it was brought home to men. To be valid it must be written on men's hearts.

But great as this discovery was, it was not complete. A covenant meant the union of two parties into a single whole. It could be carried out only when a third party had given its life, and each party had been united to the slaughtered victim (cf. Gen. xv, Ex. xxiv, 4-8, Jer. xxxiv. 18). Jeremiah did not see a victim great enough to be the covenant intermediary, uniting man and God in a valid and eternal bond; the world had to wait six hundred years, till that night when Jesus took a cup and said, " This cup is the new covenant in my blood."

CHAPTER XIII

THE LATER PROPHETS : EZEKIEL

ACCORDING to the book which bears his name, Ezekiel was a Jerusalem priest who was carried away to Babylon with Jehoiachin in 596 B.C. There he saw visions and heard the voice of Yahweh; some of the visions took him to Jerusalem, and he watched events taking place there. He recorded these, and other messages which he had to give to his fellow-exiles.

The Book of Ezekiel is quite unlike either that of Isaiah or that of Jeremiah. In structure its nearest parallel is to be found in Zechariah i-viii. It is largely composed of autobiographical prose, with a limited amount of oracular poetry, chiefly in the collection of " foreign " oracles. There is no biographical prose in all the forty-eight chapters. The style is uniform, and there are many points which suggest a Babylonian origin for the whole book.

Till quite recently the whole was accepted as being the work of Ezekiel, and the account given of his experiences was held to be correct. There were some doubts about the closing chapters, which describe in some detail a new Temple which was to be erected after the exile, and an ideal division of the land among the twelve tribes. It may be said at once that the scheme propounded by Ezekiel was quite impracticable, and this apportionment of Israelite territory is, in this respect, a strong contrast to the realistic picture he draws for the new Temple. The latter, it is true, is not always easy to follow, but we can see it clearly enough to recognise a definite and possible plan in the prophet's mind.

But during the last generation grave doubts have been ex- pressed on most of the points previously accepted as reliable. Several scholars have felt that Ezekiel could not have seen or described events which took place in Jerusalem while he him- self was in Mesopotamia. His connection with Jeremiah is difficult to explain unless he was in Jerusalem until the fall of the city in 586 B.C. Several theories have been propounded, some of them making Ezekiel much earlier than the end of the monarchy, and even placing him in northern Israel, while others would bring the book in its present form to a much later period. The most frequent type of theory is one which assumes that an original collection of oracles by " Ezekiel " has been worked over and greatly enlarged by a writer living in Babylon, while the prophet himself was confined to Palestine all through his ministry. But it is extremely difficult to find reliable criteria which enable us to distinguish between the Palestinian original and the Babylonian accretions and modifications. The prose style is so characteristic and uniform, that any theory of composite authorship requires that the later editor either imitated the style of his original basis with extraordinary skill, or that he rewrote the whole in his own natural manner. In the pages which follow, it will be assumed that, in all probability, the older tradition may be followed, and except for the actual close, the whole may be regarded as the work of a single prophet. Further, the facts of his life suggested in the book may be accepted as historical.

The following main sections may be observed.

(i) chs. i-xxiv. Prophecies concerning Judah and Jerusalem during the period 592-586 B.C.

(ii) chs. xxv-xxxii. Prophecies against foreign nations.

(iii) chs. xxxiii-xlviii. The hope and the restoration of Israel.

The first section opens with the vision in which Ezekiel receives his call to the prophetic ministry. Like many other passages this is dated, and it is assigned to the fifth year of the captivity, *i.e.* 592 B.C. Ezekiel sees Yahweh coming on His throne, and he attempts a description. All through he makes it clear that the vision is something entirely outside his experience or that of any other man. He cannot describe it accurately, because no man has ever had this experience. He has to find the nearest thing to each detail, and says repeatedly " something like . . ." The result is one of the most impressive pieces of writing in the Bible. Several of the features suggest to the prophet matters which belong to Babylonia. The strange creatures which bear the divine throne are not exactly the Mesopotamian winged bulls and lions, but they are something like them, and Ezekiel uses a word for which the nearest equivalent in modern English would be " griffin." The whole is a mass of blazing light, and at the heart of it is something which looks like brass glowing in a furnace. The smelting of brass was unknown outside Mesopotamia, and the impression made by his vision on the prophet's mind was clearly that of a brassfoundry.

In ii, 1-iii, 15 Ezekiel receives his commission; it is as if a book had been given to him and he had been compelled to swallow it. iii, 16-27 give further details of his office, stressing his responsibility as the mouthpiece of God. But he is not to speak till permission is given to him; his message must be delivered in other ways.

So in the following chapters we have a series of symbolic actions indicating the siege which Jerusalem is to endure and the desolation which will fall on the country. It is worth noting that much of this is in direct speech; presumably it was heard by Ezekiel and written down for others to read. These symbolic actions and prose oracles which predict the fate of Judah continue to the end of ch. vii.

In ch. viii the prophet is transported to Jerusalem, and there, in the Temple itself, he witnesses idolatrous forms of worship. He may have seen this sort of thing before his removal to Babylonia. In ch. ix he is shown a party of men whose task it is to destroy all the inhabitants of Jerusalem, except a few who have not shared in the false worship. Then, in ch. xi Yahweh, enthroned on the griffin-car leaves the city on its eastern side.

Ch. xii is one of those passages which have roused doubts in the minds of some modern readers. It describes, in detail, Zedekiah's attempt to escape from the doomed city, and his capture. It is felt in some quarters that this would have no meaning for Jews resident in Babylonia, and must have originated in Palestine. On the other hand there would seem to be no good reason why Ezekiel should not have announced to his fellow-exiles the events which were to take place in Judah; they would then be prepared to receive the news when it came.

xiii, 1-16 is an attack on false prophets, probably the people who were condemned by Jeremiah. Ezekiel was not the only prophet to be carried into exile; it was in the character of his message that he stood alone. The remainder of the chapter is directed against women who cast various spells on people, and in ch. xiv we have a further denunciation of the prophets;

here we have once more that terrible doctrine of the " seduced prophet " which we have already noted in Jer. xx.

A picture of the uselessness of Judah is given in ch. xv, where the nation is compared to a bit of a vine stem, never much good for practical purposes, now quite worthless because it has been charred in the fire. This is followed in ch. xvi by the story of Israel's apostasy under the figure of a loved but faithless woman. The metaphor goes back to Hosea and was used by Jeremiah in his early days but neither drew the picture with such a wealth of frightful and even loathsome detail. We cannot doubt that the prophet himself felt the horror of his words, but if he had been challenged he would have answered " Is it more horrible than sin is in the sight of God?"

Ch. xvii gives us our first glimpse of Ezekiel as a poet. In vv. 1-10 we have a picture of Zedekiah, as a sprout planted by a great eagle (Nebuchadrezzar). But it failed to turn in the right direction and was destroyed. So the last king of Judah had been false to the Chaldean power, and had intrigued with Egypt; his doom was certain. This is explained in prose, and the chapter ends with another short poem (vv. 22-24), telling of a new prince who is to rule over Judah. This Messianic passage is the first sign we have had of that belief in the restoration of Israel which later played so large a part in Ezekiel's thought.

Jeremiah had proclaimed the doctrine that men suffer for their own sins, not for those of their ancestors. This is developed by Ezekiel in ch. xviii. It is accompanied by the warning that a man's past life will not necessarily determine his fate. There is always room for a change, either for the better or for the worse. If for the better, he may be saved; if for the worse, then he must suffer the penalty for his new life of sin.

The Book of Jeremiah contains a section of oracles against the kings under whom the prophet lived (Jer. xxii). So, too, Ezekiel had something to say about the sons of Josiah, and said it in poetry. Ch. xix, 1-4 speaks of Jehoahaz, vv. 5-9 appear to begin with Jehoiakim and end with Jehoiachin. These two draw their picture from a lioness and her cubs; vv. 10-14, which may refer to Zedekiah, use the metaphor of a vine. The rest of the chapter is a summary of Israel's spiritual history, culminating in a promise of restoration if at last she will reform.

Ch. xx is a summary of the spiritual history of Israel, recording her many failures, and the sins which have led to the exile. It concludes with an appeal for her conversion, and a promise of restoration if she will give up her evil ways.

In ch. xxi the doom is nearer, and there is a wild horror in the three little songs which are included, vv. 9-13, 14-17, and 28-32. Each speaks of a sword, and while the first two are addressed to Judah, the last is concerned with Ammon. Ch. xxii is a series of threats, and in vv. 20-22 seem to contain a passage which Ezekiel has based on Jer. vi, 27-30.

Ch. xxiii reminds us of ch. xvi, and offers the same horrible picture of sin. This time, however, there are two women; one typifies northern Israel and the other Judah. The former has long since received her punishment, but her sister has not taken warning. Judah has sinned so much more than Israel, that the latter seems almost righteous by comparison.

The end is now very near, and ch. xxiv brings it before us. Vv. 3-5, 6-8, 9-14 are short poetic oracles, and vv. 15-27 are among the most pathetic passages in the Old Testament. Ezekiel loses his wife suddenly, and is told that he must refrain from any sign of mourning, as a token that Jerusalem is falling, and the people in Babylon will be unable to mourn for the city they loved. Here we get a view of Ezekiel which is entirely fresh. From the fierceness of his denunciations we should never have suspected the tenderness which lay below the surface, and we learn something of the mental agony which he must have experienced whenever the truth about Jerusalem and Judah came home to him. With the fall of Jerusalem he is released from the embargo laid on his speech at his call, and henceforward he can freely utter his message.

As in several other prophetic books, we have a collection of oracles uttered against foreign nations. It occupies chs. xxv-xxxii : First come the peoples who were near neighbours of Israel, and gloated over her fall, sometimes occupying territory left desolate by war and deportation. They include Ammon (xxv, 1-7), Moab (xxv, 8-11), Edom (xxv, 12-14), and Philistia (xxv, 15-17). These are all small peoples, most of them less powerful than Judah herself But with ch. xxvi begins an attack on Tyre, perhaps the greatest commercial city of the ancient world. The collection continues down to xxviii, 19, and is followed by a single piece dealing with Sidon. The

Tyrian section proper contains a number of oracles, mostly in verse form, and some of these are among the most splendid pieces of poetry which the Old Testament contains. We have for example, the figure of Tyre as a great ship in ch. xxvii, and that of the Griffin in the garden of God (xxviii, 11-19). It is to be noted that these poems are much longer than the average prophetic oracle, and show signs of artistic composition. They are not simply the swift outbursts of tense emotion which we normally find in the prophetic books. The last enemy threatened is Egypt, and again we have a series of oracles, some in prose and others in verse. The latter are nearer to the normal type than the longer poems against Tyre, but sometimes reach a high lyrical standard. They are contained in chs. xxix-xxxii; like the Tyre collection, that devoted to Egypt includes prose passages as well as poems.

Ch. xxxiii begins the last section of the book, that in which Ezekiel looks into the future and sees the restoration of Israel. It opens with a section which strongly recalls passages which are found in the earlier part of the book. Thus in xxxiii, 1-9 the prophet receives a commission and a warning of his responsibility. xxxiii, 12-20 recall ch. xviii, and the next two verses tell of the survivor who brought to the prophet the news that Jerusalem had fallen. Ch. xxxiv is distinctly Messianic; Israel's rulers in the past have been selfish and careless shepherds, but a new Israel shall be governed by a new David; indeed it is Yahweh Himself who is to tend them, giving them justice and prosperity.

Ch. xxxv is an attack on Edom. It seems out of place here, but was probably included in the third division of the book rather than in the second, because it formed a preliminary to the restored Israel. Judah suffered more from Edom than from any other people in her immediate neighbourhood. The two nations had been bitterly hostile to one another at least since the time of David, and the historian would throw a large part of the blame on Judah. But when the land was desolated by Nebuchadrezzar and the last remnants of an organised community had fled to Egypt, the southern tribe moved northwards and occupied the richer land of southern Judah. The expulsion of these semi-nomad immigrants seemed to men like Ezekiel to be a necessary preliminary to the full restoration of Israel in her ancestral home.

It is with ch. xxxvi that we begin the story of the coming

restoration. There is no glossing over the sin which has led to the exile; the message is rather that of Is xl, 2. Ezekiel had learnt, too, from Jeremiah, and, like him, had seen that a valid restoration must be based on a spiritual revolution. So Israel is to have a new heart (xxxvi. 22-32) and so to prepare for the glorious future which awaits her.

This future is typified by the resurrection of dry bones scattered over a wide plain (ch. xxxvii), one of the best-known passages in the book. In chs. xxxviii, xxxix we have a picture of what will happen if and when the wild northern tribes break into Palestine as they did in the last quarter of the seventh century. " Gog," however, seems to be a personal name, and some scholars would identify him with Gyges of Lydia or some other prince of the northern lands.

Ezekiel was a priest, and for him the restoration of the Temple and its ritual was essential to the life of the new Israel. He therefore gives a detailed picture of the new Temple, presumably based on his memories of the old, followed by certain items of ritual (chs. xl-xlvi). The picture ends with the vision of the great river which is to flow south-eastward from the sanctuary (xlvii, 1-12). The remainder, xlvii, 13-xlviii, 23, gives a sketch of an ideal division of the land between the tribes. Only western Palestine is considered, and the scheme simply draws straight lines across the map from east to west. This can hardly be the work of a realist like Ezekiel, and its tone is strongly in contrast with the view of the restored Temple. It is not surprising that many scholars regard it as the work of a later hand; xlvii, 12 makes a fine conclusion to a great book.

What has Ezekiel to say to the world? The most striking feature of the book is expressed in the sentence " that they may know that I am Yahweh." He believes supremely in Yahweh as the ruler of the whole world, and all history must illustrate the truth. It is perhaps this, as much as the prophet's temperament, which gives him an air of sternness, even of rigidity. All the prophets had severe things to say, but none was more outspoken, we might almost say fiercer, than Ezekiel. It may be that his very horror at human sin drove him into violent speech; we know that he was capable of deep and sincere affection, and the same fervour which showed itself in passionate devotion to his wife had another side, and was no less passionate in rebuking wrong. In any case he offers a strong contrast to his gentle, but broken-hearted master, Jeremiah.

From that master he learned one of his most important doctrines, the meaning of the individual in religion. He had a strong faith in the invariable action of Yahweh's laws; sin must always be followed by punishment. There could be no escape, except through repentance and conversion, and though he allowed for free will, his doctrine was in other respects every whit as rigid as the *karma* of the Indian philosopher.

It was just here that he was saved from absolute pessimism by his insistence on the individual. On the old view, the nation was composed not merely of those who were living at any particular time, but of all successive generations, past, present, and future. Men explained their disasters by reference to the sins of their fathers. There is, of course, much truth in this point of view, but it is only natural that a pioneer of a new factor should overstress his fresh discovery. On the old hypothesis the sins of the fathers, *e.g.* in the time of Manasseh, must have meant the complete disappearance of the Israelite people. But Ezekiel's individualism gave each generation a fresh opportunity. It was not bound by the acts of its predecessors, but started with a clean record. It could follow its own path, either to happiness or ruin. It could make a complete break with the past, and, in spite of all that had gone before, construct for itself a life of genuine consecration to Yahweh. There was always hope, not in a change of Yahweh's principles and will, but in the new generation which was springing up.

The great hope of the future manifests itself in one very striking way. Ezekiel could not believe in the final disunion of Israel. A century and a half had elapsed since Samaria had fallen, and the northern tribes had been wiped off the roll of the people. But in the ideal state which was to come they would be restored, and once more take their place with their fellows in the new nation. We need not rely on the last section of the book for evidence of this belief; Ezekiel so often speaks of Israel when he is depicting the happy future. The very name of Judah occurs only some half dozen times in xxv-xlvii, 12, while that of Israel appears in about eighty places in these chapters. Above all we have such passages as that of the two sticks in ch. xxxvii. To Ezekiel the whole people was one and indivisible, and he could look forward to the time when the lost tribes should be found again, and united once more into a great flock, under the one divine shepherd.

CHAPTER XIV

THE LATER PROPHETS : THE BOOK OF THE TWELVE

UNDER this head we have the group which is often called today that of the " Minor Prophets," though one or two of them are most important. They include the earliest and the latest of our prophetic books, and though none of them runs to more than fourteen chapters, several of them are far more significant than the mere length of their surviving prophecies would suggest. The order of the books is the same as that which we find in our English Bibles, and it is clear that the number twelve was reached deliberately by the attachment of anonymous collections to those which bore the name of a prophet. We will note these instances as we come to them.

Hosea. The Book of Hosea stands first in this collection, though he was not quite the earliest of the prophets included in it. He belonged entirely to the northern kingdom, and lived through its last years. It is even possible that some of his utterances may come from the days which immediately followed the fall of Samaria in 721, and, in any case, we can hardly date any of his work before 740 B.C.

Hosea is one of the few men of the Old Testament who have allowed us to see and to share his inner life. His whole outlook was coloured, and in some sense controlled, by his domestic experiences. We have two accounts of his marriage, one in ch. i and one in ch. iii. The two have frequently been read together, as if they had been intended to form a connected story. This, however, is improbable, since ch. i belongs to the biographical type of writing, while ch. iii is in that autobiographical prose which we have observed in the three longer books. There are, then, three possible interpretations of the facts : (i) the two passages may refer to two different women, (ii) they may record two stages in the prophet's relations with the same woman, (iii) they may give two different accounts of the same events (ch. iii, however, contains no mention of any children). It is the second of these three which has captured the imagination of most modern readers, and it is not impossible that it is the right explanation, though this cannot be stated with certainty. According to this view, Hosea married a woman of bad character, though he may not have known what she was. Three children were born, and received symbolic names, much as Isaiah's sons had done. The woman left her husband and gave herself up to a life of immorality, sinking at length into actual slavery. But, in spite of all he had suffered, Hosea still loved her, and could not rest till he had found her and bought her back to his own home, where she was at length restored to her old position.

Another interpretation of the recorded facts depicts Gomer as a sacred prostitute, attached to one of the northern temples. Unfortunately there can be no doubt that such persons existed; they seem to have been a regular feature of the old Canaanite religion, and were almost certainly introduced into Israelite sanctuaries along with other forms of corrupt ritual. In Mesopotamia such women were allowed to leave the temple after a period of service, to marry, and to settle down in a normal home. Presumably a price would have to be paid by the man who married such a woman, and there would naturally be a period of seclusion before the actual marriage, to allow the " sanctity " of the woman to wear off.

But, whether either of these reconstructions is right or not, one fact is certain; Hosea loved his wife passionately, and knew that she was unfaithful to him. This gave form to his message. In his own experience he saw a reflection of the love felt by Yahweh for His people, His appalling sorrow at their faithlessness and apostasy, and the price He was prepared to pay to win them back.

In ch. xi we have another picture of divine love. It is that of a father, whose tenderness for his child knows no limits. He has taught the little toddler to walk, and, in spite of the son's waywardness and rejection, He still loves the boy and longs for his return. We think inevitably of the prodigal son; indeed, to many of us Hosea seems to be the most completely Christian of the prophets.

Hosea was not blind to the political and social conditions of his time; indeed no man in his position could be. He saw one king follow another, usually by assassinating his predecessor; after Jeroboam II only one king of northern Israel left the crown to his son. He could not escape the sense of the

Assyrian peril, and strongly condemned the statesmen of Samaria for thinking that they could save their people by intriguing with the great king or with Egypt. Nothing but a total revolution in heart could save Israel in his day, and yet the love of Yahweh was so great that He would wait to the very last.

Like other prophetic books, **Hosea** seems to be composed of two or more collections. We may compare the structure of the book of Jeremiah, where the compiler has prefixed a prose passage to each of the oracular collections which he reproduced. Ch. ii forms a characteristic short collection, with several oracles linked together by a common subject, and a happy ending. Chs. iv*ff.* may have been a single collection but it is also possible that two or more have been put together; the compiler may have had no prose material except what he has given us in chs. i and iii. Certainly the opening verses of ch. xi suggest the beginning of a fresh collection.

There is little doubt about the unity of authorship in this book. From first to last it breathes the same passionate and intense spirit, offers the same telling staccato style, and gives the impression generally of emanating from the same personality. Some scholars have felt that the few hopeful passages are inconsistent with Hosea's attitude and teaching and must be due to a later hand. But a moment's reflection will suggest that this is by no means a necessary deduction from the facts. On the contrary, Hosea knew what his own love meant, and from that knowledge deduced the infinitely greater love of God for His own people. The higher the love, the stronger the hope, and this prophet's message would have been incomplete if he had ignored the possibility that even the worst of sinners might be redeemed.

In a few cases reference is made to Judah. Here there is some reason for suspecting later insertion, since obviously Hosea's message was directed to the northern kingdom. No oracle is expressly concerned with Judah alone, as some of Isaiah's utterances deal only with the northern kingdom, and where the name of Judah occurs it may well be a minor interpolation, two or three words only, or even a deliberate modification of the text. The substantial unity of the book is not affected by these passages.

Hosea is not an easy book to read. The prophet's style is peculiar and at times elusive. Some of the oracles seem to

H

have been mutilated before they came into the hands of the collectors. Further, the text has suffered much in course of transmission, and in many places is unintelligible as it stands; translators either emend conjecturally or write words which appear to have little meaning. In spite of these difficulties, however, we can, with careful study, get a clear picture of what the prophet had to tell his people and us. None repays such labour so fully and completely as does Hosea.

Joel. Every prophetic book has its own peculiarities, but Joel is one of the strangest. In a sense it is hardly prophecy at all. In many ways it belongs to the category of Apocalypse rather than to that of prophecy. It draws a picture of the end which is to come on the established order. Monstrous divine agents appear, to work ruin and destruction on earth. They are described as locusts, but belong to no recognisable species. It is possible that the prophet's imagination was stirred by an actual swarm which had desolated the land. Certainly i, 1-14, 16-20, ii, 12-19, 21-27, read like a narrative of desolation caused by such an actual swarm, together with the call to prayer and the subsequent promise of recovery.

There are wide differences of opinion as to the date of Joel. Some scholars would regard this as the oldest of our prophetic books; others think it is one of the latest, if not the latest of all. There are no references to contemporary events, and no suggestion that the monarchy is still in existence.

Amos is the earliest of the canonical prophets. His work was done during the last period of prosperity in Israel, the reign of Jeroboam II. Though his home was in the far south of Judah, his prophecies were addressed almost entirely to the northern kingdom. He belonged to one of those areas in which agriculture was difficult if not impossible, and still retained the outlook and simplicity of the nomad period. It will be remembered that Elijah also came from a similar district to the east of the Jordan, and there is a certain likeness between the two. Both are rugged characters, looking on the more complicated civilisation of agricultural and civic Palestine from the outside. Unlike Hosea and Jeremiah, they sit in judgment on a community in which they have no share or part. They can see clearly what is wrong, and condemn it, but they do not feel that agony of remorse for the sins of Israel which is so marked a feature of the two just mentioned.

Amos is one of our most important sources for the actual

history of Israel in the later years of the monarchy. He does not, it is true, give us any account of events which took place, except, probably, in vi, 13, where we should read, with a slight change of the vowels : " Ye which rejoice over Lo-debar, which say, Have we not taken Karnaim by our own strength?" Lo-debar and Karnaim are important places to the east of the Jordan, in the area which Jeroboam recovered from the Syrians. But Amos does depict the general condition of the country, and fills in the picture sketched in outline by Isaiah and others. Thus we have Isaiah complaining of the way in which the wealthy gathered all the land into large estates (Is. v, 8-10). Amos shows us the sufferings of the poor man, now reduced from the position of the free peasant cultivating his ancestral plot—a man like Naboth—to that of a rack-rented tenant farmer or even a serf. He sketches the gross luxury and selfishness of the rich man, who made his home in a city and lived a life of indulgence and ease, but was utterly careless of the poor wretches who supplied him with his pleasures.

Amos foresees the ruin of the nation. Some scholars believe that he was aware of the growing power of Assyria, and that the great eastern empire was already threatening the inde-pendence, indeed the life, of all lesser states. But this seems unlikely, for it was not till the advent of Tiglath-pileser III in 745 that Assyria began to recover from the depression into which she had gradually fallen during the last half century. On the surface all was well in Amos' days, and in viii, 9 we have a remark which has suggested to many that the prophet had recently witnessed an eclipse of the sun. This can only have been that which occurred in June 763, twenty years before the revival of Assyria. Amos saw more deeply into the meaning of history; if a community allowed itself to split into two clearly divided sections, one consisting of a few wealthy people, and the other presenting a mass of hopeless, grinding poverty, then its doom is certain. Either it will perish by internal explosion, as French society did at the end of the eighteenth century and Russian early in the twentieth, or it will become an easy prey to the first serious invader who attacks it. When Israel was a country of Naboths, she had successfully resisted the assault of Shalmaneser III at Karkar (853 B.C.); in 734 B.C. she could offer only a nominal resist-ance to Tiglath-pileser. A nation which has lost its spiritual co-efficient, its personal vigour, is as surely perishing as the caterpillar in whose body an ichneumon fly has laid its egg.

Amos found no help in the religion of the people he watched. There was plenty of religiosity, but no true religion. Temple ritual was observed with meticulous care, but it included features like sacramental prostitution, which we have already noticed in thinking of Hosea. Nor was it in any sense a guardian of morality, rather the opposite. A religious act like sleeping in a temple could be made an excuse for disregarding the humane law which compelled a creditor to let his debtor have back for the night a garment taken in pledge. Sabbath observance merely gave the rascally shopkeeper more chance to plan his knaveries. The courts of justice were venal; a small bribe—a pair of shoes would be enough—might make it possible for the rich man to secure a verdict which would hand over the poor as a slave. The only hope was a complete return to the old Mosaic principles which had been maintained in the outlying parts of the land, and revert to the pure faith and practice of nomad days.

The book of Amos contains all three recognised types of writing. Most of it is in the form of poetic oracle, but there is one passage (vii, 10-17) which is the work of a biographer, and in chs. vii-ix we have a series of visions in which the prophet describes his own experiences. The book falls into three parts. In 1, 3-ii, 5 we have a collection of oracles against foreign nations, Damascus, Gaza, Tyre, Edom, Ammon, Moab and Judah. These are cast in a peculiar form; all have the same framework, and differ only in the offence for which the people is condemned, and, to a lesser extent, in the punishment threatened. We may conclude that this formula : " For three transgressions of X, yea for four, I will not turn back its punishment " was normal with Amos.

He uses the same formula (or is it prefixed by the compiler?) when introducing the first oracle in the second section, which is concerned with the sins of Israel. The third division includes the " visions "; several of these are used to introduce short oracles.

The greater part of the book is generally recognised as containing genuine utterances of Amos. One or two of the oracles against foreign nations have been challenged, mainly on the ground that they do not fit into the general scheme, but the only one which rouses serious doubts is the last, that directed against Judah (ii, 4-5). Here we have no specific crime, but only a general accusation of failure to observe the law of Yahweh. This is unlike Amos; elsewhere he gives concrete examples of the sins he denounces. More serious is the feeling that the conclusion, ix, 8b-15, is the work of one or more later writers. It consists almost entirely of hopeful predictions, and ix, 11-12 certainly presupposes the end of the Davidic dynasty, i.e. it is exilic or post-exilic. There is little in the earlier chapters to suggest that Amos himself had any real hope of reform and recovery, while we are familiar with the tendency of compilers to finish their books with happy endings.

Obadiah. This, the shortest book in the Old Testament, consists of a single small collection against one foreign people, the Edomites. Two of these are also found in Jeremiah xlix; Ob. 1-4 is nearly identical with Jer. xlix, 14-16, and the differences throw a strong light on the corruptions which arise in course of transmission. It would seem that in most instances of variation the Jeremiah text is to be preferred. Ob. 5, also, appears to be composed of phrases taken from an oracle which we find in a more complete state in Jer. xlix, 7-11.

We know nothing of Obadiah beyond what this little book has to say to us. Even his name (it means simply " Servant of Yahweh ") may be a later description of an unknown prophet. Some of the oracles suggest a time not long after the fall of Jerusalem, and may well have been uttered by Jeremiah himself. But there can be no certainty on either the date or the personality of the prophet(s) to whom we owe these oracles.

Jonah. Here again, we have a book which is unique among our prophets. It consists almost entirely of narrative about the prophet whose name it bears. It includes a Psalm attributed to him, but this has no reference to the message he has to give. Only a single sentence records his actual preaching : " Yet forty days, and Nineveh shall be overthrown " (iii, 4). The real lesson of the book, then, must be sought in the man and his actions rather than in his teaching.

The story is one of the most familiar in the Old Testament. Called to denounce Nineveh for its sins, Jonah shirks the duty laid upon him, and tries to escape from Yahweh by sea. His efforts are futile, a great storm endangers the ship and all on board, and Jonah is thrown into the sea, where a great fish swallows him. He is thrown up on the land, and this time carries out his orders. At his preaching, the people of Nineveh repent. Meanwhile Jonah has retired to a point outside the city, from which he can watch the fulfilment of his prediction. He is overcome by the heat, and a gourd grows over him and protects him from the sun. But it withers, and the forty days pass without trouble for the city. Jonah is bitterly angry and complains to God that he has been deceived, as he had feared. The answer is that he himself has sorrowed for the withering of an ephemeral plant, and shall not God have pity on a great city with all its human and animal inhabitants?

Obviously the interest of the book lies in its interpretation. Jesus quoted it in rebuking the Jews of His day, and one form of the Gospel tradition thought of Jonah's three days and nights in the fish as a forecast of the three days and two nights during which the body of Jesus lay in the tomb. In general there have been two main lines of interpretation. One takes the story quite literally, and tends to concentrate on Jonah's miraculous deliverance. The other view, while not denying the possibility of the miracle, feels that stress on this element in the story misses the truth which it is designed to illustrate. That is, surely, the love and pity of God for sinful men, even though they may be outside the people of the Covenant.

An extreme form of this theory makes the whole book an allegory. Jonah is the Jewish people, called to an evangelical mission for the whole world. They refuse to accept their duty and are swallowed up in the exile. Incidentally it is pointed out that a " fish " was the symbol of Nineveh. Israel returned from the exile, and its commission was renewed. But the nation was still jealous of its privileges and was unwilling to allow the possibility that any Gentiles could be saved. On this hypothesis the book will be a protest against the narrowness and exclusiveness of post-exilic Judah.

It is difficult to define the date of the book. The prophet is apparently identified with a certain Jonah mentioned in II Kings xiv, 25, though there it is not clear whether the man lived actually in the reign of Jeroboam II or whether he had predicted the restoration of Israel at some earlier period. But in any case, he can hardly have been the hero of this book. The description given of the great city is accurate for the latest period of its history. But the combination of three cities into one, which gave Nineveh its great size, did not take place till long after the time of Jeroboam II. On the allegorical view, of course, the book must be post-exilic. A case for the later date would be strengthened if we regarded the Psalm in ch. ii as a part of the original book. But it looks as if it were a later insertion. It does not altogether fit the conditions of a man who is still living in the belly of a fish, and it consists largely of phrases found in other Psalms. In such cases there can be little doubt that the Jonah Psalm is the borrower; Pss. xlii, l, lxix and cxx are laid under contribution.

But whatever view we hold of the authorship, date, and structure of this book, its message of a world-wide offer of forgiveness and salvation is valid for all time and for all peoples.

Micah. The Book of Micah has the unique distinction of being quoted verbatim in another prophetic book. The last verses of ch. iii were used by the champions of Jeremiah in saving that prophet from the religious leaders who were offended by his utterances (Jer. xxvi, 18). As this passage is little more than a century later than Micah himself, we may take it as satisfactory evidence of his authorship, at least of chs. i-iii.

The mention of Hezekiah in Jer. xxvi, 19 also attests the date given at the head of the book, and shows us that Micah was a contemporary of Hosea and of Isaiah. But his situation is very different from theirs. Hosea was a man of the city, and lived amid the collapsing northern kingdom. Isaiah was also a man of the city, but was a frequenter of the king's court, and was concerned with international politics as well as with the sufferings of his own people. In some ways Micah is nearer to Amos than any other prophet, but there is one important difference between the two. The older man saw the sufferings of the peasant from the outside; Micah was himself under the harrow, for he belonged to the fertile country between the central range of hills and the sea. There is a bitterness, almost a savagery about his utterances which goes beyond that of any other prophet. They could be fierce in denunciation, but none was so fierce as this low-born peasant from the border land between Judah and Philistia.

This man writes in a style all his own. In i, 10ff. we have an oracle marked by puns on almost all the places he mentions. In ii, 9f. we have a vivid and heartrending picture of an eviction, and we have few more powerful metaphors of oppression than that of iii, 2f., where the greedy oppressor strips the flesh from the bones of his victim, grinds his bones, and throws all into the stock-pot. Even Amos had never talked like this, so far as we know.

The reference in Jer. xxvi has seemed to many scholars to imply that Micah said nothing to qualify his denunciation or to hold out hope of recovery from the punishment due. There is, then, a widespread feeling that his original prophecies end with ch. iii, and that what follows is the work of a later prophet. Ch. iv opens with a passage which we find, in a less complete form, at the head of Isaiah ii. The chapters which follow have a much brighter tone than chs. i-iii. In v, 1-3 we have the well-known prediction of the birth of the Messiah at Bethlehem, followed by a passage which certainly looks as if it came from the age of Micah, even if it is the work of another prophet. One other passage deserves special mention. This is vi, 6-8, apparently modelled on the kind of ritual dialogue which would be observed by a worshipper coming to offer sacrifice in a temple. The enquirer asks the priest for direction as to the right kind of sacrifice which he is to offer for the removal of sin. This may have been normal, but it is difficult to imagine a sanctuary priest giving the same answer as the prophet. No victim, however costly, will avail; what Yahweh requires is that man shall do justly, love " mercy, ' and walk humbly with his God. We might have here a summary of the teaching given by Amos, Hosea and Isaiah, and many people feel that this is one of the greatest utterances in the Old Testament.

In some quarters it is felt that a division should be made at the end of ch. v, and that chs. iv-v and vi-vii form separate collections. The reasons for this arrangement are by no means so strong as those which have led scholars to conclude that the prophecies of Micah end with ch. iii. But whoever was responsible in the first place for these four chapters, they include passages which we must count among the most valuable that the Old Testament has enshrined for us.

Nahum. The Book of Nahum opens with an alphabetic Psalm. That is to say, each verse begins with a special letter of the alphabet, the letters being taken in their natural order. We have several other examples of this arrangement in Lamentations and in the Psalter, and there are various forms, more or less complicated. In this case the acrostic is not carried all through the Psalm, either because the poet found it too difficult or because the text has suffered in course of transmission.

The Psalm serves as an introduction to a remarkable book. Nahum has nothing to say about the sins of Israel or Judah, and offers neither punishment nor hope to his people. He is solely concerned with the approaching fall of Nineveh, which was captured and destroyed by Babylonians and Medes in 612 B.C. Since this event is predicted, the prophecy must be earlier than its date, though it need not be much earlier. It possibly owes its preservation to its magnificent style. As he gloats over the coming ruin of the tyrant city, the prophet breaks into stirring and vivid language; his picture of the sack of Nineveh has few parallels in sacred or profane literature. But he has little to add to our knowledge of God.

Habakkuk. This little book has an importance out of all proportion to its length. Like the Book of Nahum, it contains two chapters of prophecy and a Psalm. Here, however, the Psalm comes at the end and not at the beginning. It has, too, some of those characteristic marks which we find elsewhere only in the Psalter. There are musical directions at the end and a " title " at the beginning; the mysterious term " Selah " occurs only here outside the Psalter. The subject is not relevant to the prophet's message; we have here a hymn of praise in which the power of Yahweh is celebrated.

Among the newly discovered documents found in the Jordan valley there is a commentary on this book. It deals, however, only with chs. i-ii, as though the commentator did not regard ch. iii as an original part of the book. He may, on the other hand, have said nothing about it because he was writing with a special object, and the Psalm did not lend itself to his purpose. It is not impossible that this passage was originally included in the Psalter, and was removed from it in order to link it up with other material ascribed to Habakkuk.

At first sight it appears that the book offers us a serious problem. When did the prophet live and work, and to what events does he refer? In i, 6-11 we have a reference to the Chaldeans, with special stress on their character as terrible invaders. In the three preceding verses we find a general complaint of injustice and cruelty; if we had to read the two passages as consecutive parts of a single whole, we should have to regard the Chaldeans as the instruments of Yahweh's vengeance. Yet in i,11 they seem to be condemned as the oppressors of the people. Moreover, in the latter part of the book the great criminal seems to be an individual, not a nation.

Various suggestions have been made to meet the difficulties of interpretation. Some have suggested changing the order, and putting i, 5-11 after ii, 4. Others alter the text and make Alexander the Great the real villain of the piece. But the general tone and such reference as we have suggest rather the age of Jeremiah. The denunciation of the tyrant in ii, 12*f.* (v. 14 seems to have been suggested by Is. xi, 9) is very like what Jeremiah had said about Jehoiakim (*cf.* Jer. xxii, 13*ff.*), though this is not a mere case of an oracle found in two different books.

The general conclusion, then, would seem to be that Habakkuk worked during the reign of Jehoiakim, probably soon after the battle of Carchemish (605 B.C.). In so far as the tyrant is a foreign power other than the Chaldeans, we may think of Egypt, and the cruel individual may be Jehoiakim.

These matters, however, are largely external to the main problem raised in the book. That is what we commonly call the problem of suffering, or rather the problem of the moral justice or injustice involved in the distribution of suffering. The book opens with a short complaint (i, 2-4), and the question is clearly stated in i, 13 : " Too pure of eyes art thou to look on evil, and thou canst not gaze on oppression. Why, then, dost thou gaze on the treacherous, when the wicked swallows up the man who is more righteous than he?"

Here is a question which has puzzled humanity ever since the days of Habakkuk. Jeremiah had felt it (*cf.* Jer. xii, 1), but had put it on one side when confronted with urgent personal problems. It may be stated quite simply : There is much suffering in the world which is not deserved by the sufferers, and many who are prosperous are steeped in crime of all kinds. Either, then, God is not the supreme ruler of the universe, or He is not just in His distribution of rewards and punishments.

Two remarks may be made at once. Such a problem could not have been raised unless God had been presented as both omnipotent and righteous. There is no problem for the polytheist because some of his gods are good and some evil.

Still less is it a problem for the animist, for the objects of his worship are usually malicious and dangerous. It is only men with high conceptions of deity, men like the great prophets of Israel, who find a problem here, for a problem arises only when a theory is contradicted by a fact of experience.

In the second place, as soon as the prophetic conception of God had been stated and accepted, the problem was bound to arise and demand solution. No completely satisfactory answer to Habakkuk's question has yet been given, and it may be for ever beyond the grasp of a finite intelligence. Christianity alone has thrown real light on the problem by its insistence on the fact that God Himself endures suffering through the evil done by human beings. There must, then, be a reason for it, an answer to the question, even if it be at present unattainable by the mind of man.

Habakkuk at least found some practical answer: " The righteous shall live by his fidelity." In other words, if a man will only maintain right relations with God, he will find in the end that the pain he has thought to be evil is really in full harmony with his belief in an all-powerful and a wholly good God. This may be no solution of the problem from an intellectual point of view, but it does offer a method by which the sufferer may win practical experience of the truth that there is a solution, and that God knows what He is doing.

Zephaniah. Prophets were drawn from all classes of society. In Amos we have the shepherd, in Hosea the common townsman, in Micah the peasant, in Jeremiah and Ezekiel the priests, and in Isaiah the courtier and statesman. In Zephaniah, to judge from the long genealogy, we have a member of the royal house. Yet it must be admitted that his contribution to our religious thinking is secondary to that of his great predecessors and contemporaries.

The period of Zephaniah's activity is placed in the reign of Josiah. His oracles are all threats of destruction, not only on Judah and Jerusalem, but also on other peoples, Philistia (ii, 4-7), Moab and Ammon (ii, 8-11), " Kush," i.e. Ethiopia or Egypt (ii, 12), and Assyria (ii, 13-14). Then we have a picture of nations collected for judgment and destruction in iii, 8-10. The whole is strongly eschatological, and the tone is set in such passages as that describing the Day of Yahweh (i, 14-18). We know that in 626 B.C. Judah was threatened by hordes of savage invaders from the north, and their coming may have stirred the prophetic spirit in both Jeremiah and Zephaniah. The eighth and seventh century prophets did not ignore eschatology, but in no other do we get such a picture of the *Dies irae*.

Haggai. Most of the prophets whom we have been considering did their work before or during the exile. The last three prophetic books seem to belong wholly to the restored community. Each of the five utterances ascribed to Haggai is accurately dated, and all are placed within a period of a few months in the year 522 B.C.

The book is entirely in prose, and the third person is always used. But this is not the normal biographical prose, for we hear nothing of the prophet's experiences; only his words are given to us. It is at least possible that originally the first person was employed, and that the change to the third was made by a later editor.

Sixteen years had passed since the first decree of Cyrus had authorised the rebuilding of the Temple in Jerusalem. But nothing had been done. The people were few and poor, struggling for bare existence in a desolate land. Even when they began to recover and erect good houses for themselves, they neglected the work for which they had originally come back from Babylonia. It was Haggai's task to rouse them to a sense of their duty, and he was so far successful that in ii, 18 we hear that the foundations were actually laid.

We note at once the strong contrast between Haggai and his predecessors. The Temple and its ritual were matters of supreme importance to him.

It seems clear from the closing section of the book (ii, 20-23) that Haggai was looking forward to the establishment of a Messianic kingdom in Judah, and possibly he encouraged Zerubbabel to plan a revolt from Persia.

Zechariah. The last two books of the Prophetic canon are those of Zechariah and Malachi. Their structure, however, suggests that we have here the work of more than two prophets. In Zech. i-vi we have a series of visions described in the first person. These are immediately followed by a few direct predictions in chs. vii and viii. The whole is in autobiographical prose, and has a uniform and characteristic style. Then come three small collections of oracular matter (some of it in prose), each headed with the word " Massa," literally " burden," but frequently used of prophetic speech. A name has been found for the last of these, taken from the actual text, and we know it as the Book of Malachi. The word means " my messenger," and occurs in Mal. iii, 1. But the other two, having no names attached to them, were simply appended to the eighth chapter of Zechariah, which thus falls into three parts.

The original Zechariah (*i.e.* the prophet of Zech. i-viii) was a contemporary of Haggai, and worked with him in stirring up the returned Jews to renew their Temple. The book opens with an exhortation to repentance, and this followed by the first of the visions (i,7-17). Here the prophet sees a man standing in a myrtle grove, and messengers come riding up to him, and report that the whole earth is quiet. There follows the divine promise of help and restoration for Judah and Jerusalem. The vision is dated in the year 522 B.C. and it is impossible to read it without feeling an atmosphere of mystery and wonder. In this, as in later visions, the prophet has with him a person whom he calls " the angel who spoke in me "; he is conscious that the divine voice is talking to him, but the experience seems to be less like that of normal audition than it is with other prophets.

The second vision (i,18-21) brings before the prophet four horns, which symbolise the nations who have scattered Israel and Judah. They are followed by four smiths, whose task it is to terrify nations into a state of terror and overthrow them. This vision is undated, but our experience of collections in other prophets makes it uncertain whether all the visions are granted on the same day.

In the third vision the prophet sees a man with a measuring line, going out to mark the boundaries of the city (ii, 1-13). But he is told that Jerusalem is to have no walls. In the first place her population will be too large to be enclosed, and in the second place Yahweh Himself will be all round her and protect her. Strictly speaking, the vision occupies only the first five verses; the rest of the chapter contains predictions of the good time coming.

The fourth vision (iii, 1-10) is particularly interesting for several reasons. It illustrates the prophet's anxiety to have a truly purified worship in the new Temple, and it introduces a figure who is much more familiar outside the Old Testament than in it. Zechariah witnesses a trial scene. Joshua, the high priest, is standing before Yahweh, dressed in the foul garments normally assumed by a person accused of crime. His accuser is " the Satan," who is yet a long way from the Devil of whom we hear in the New Testament. He resembles the Satan of the opening chapters of Job; he is an official of the court of God, whose function it is to bring before the divine judgment seat persons whom he believes to be guilty of some offence. We are taken into the court at the moment when the sentence is pronounced in favour of the accused, and Joshua is given his robes, clean and pure, while the official mitre is placed on his head. He thus has the proper authentication of God Himself, and is declared fit to carry out the duties of the high priest.

All the visions take place by night, the fifth (iv, 1-14) begins with Zechariah waking from a kind of slumber, and seeing the lampstand of the Temple, with its seven branches. Oil is supplied by two olive trees (some commentators regard these as a later addition), which pour into the lamps a continuous stream of fuel. The interpretation is less obvious than in the other visions, but the " angel " explains that the vision is an encouragement to Zerubbabel to carry on his work. He may have neither might nor power, but the Spirit of God will be with him and see that his work ends in triumph.

Ch. v contains two visions. The first (v, 1-4) shows a great scroll, full of destructive curses, flying through the air. This carries the condemnation of the wicked, who are to be eliminated from the new community. Just as its priesthood is to be holy, so its laity must be pure and free from crime.

In v, 5-11 we have a vision closely connected with the former. A large vessel with a leaden cover appears, and a woman is sitting in it. Two other women, furnished with stork's wings, lift it up and carry it to Babylonia. The explanation is that this is Wickedness, who is to be removed altogether from Judah and go to her own place.

The last of the visions is contained in ch. vi, 1-8. Zechariah sees four chariots emerging from a valley between two mountains. They are drawn by horses of different colours, and they go towards the four quarters of the earth. One is singled out; it is that which is drawn by black horses, and it goes towards Babylon, carrying the message that the whole earth is quiet.

When we take this series of visions together, it seems clear that the prophet has in view the coming of a Messianic kingdom, probably thinking of Zerubbabel as the Messiah; he is to rule jointly with the high priest Joshua. In the new order there is to be no distinction between secular and religious. So at the end of the list comes a symbolic action which gives a sign. The prophet has to make two crowns and place them on the head of Joshua. That, at least, is the form which our text takes today, but many scholars think that the name of Zerubbabel has either dropped out or has been replaced by that of the priest.

Chs. vii and viii stand apart from the series of visions. They are dated two years later, i.e. in 518 B.C., and are concerned with the new time. Here we have a series of normal prose utterances, beginning with a question about fasting (vii, 1-3). The answer is that the true fast should be ethical and not ritual; the spirit of the pre-exilic prophets is not dead, though it has naturally been overlaid by interest in the Messianic future (vii, 4-14). The whole Zechariah collection ends with a picture of the new age, in which fasting has given place to rejoicing.

We now come to the first of the three short collections bearing the title " Massa." It consists of a series of oracles, mostly in poetic form, beginning with threats to Phoenicia and Philistia (ix, 1-8). This is followed by a description of the triumphal entry of the Messiah into Jerusalem (ix, 9-17), a passage which has become familiar to us from its use in the New Testament story. It is possible that we have two oracles here, both in verse, the second beginning with v, 13. The date is disputed; some scholars believe that the mention of Greece in v. 13 implies a Maccabaean origin; others think that the name is a later insertion.

The remainder of this short collection is taken up with denunciation of the people's leaders, the " shepherds," who are to be replaced by Yahweh Himself. There are several short poetic oracles, and an interesting passage in autobiographical prose (xi, 4-16). The section has been referred by some scholars to the Maccabaean age, and the " shepherds " have been identified with the corrupt high priests who collaborated with Antiochus Epiphanes in his attempt to hellenise the Jewish people and religion. The prophet seems to have been influenced by Ezekiel, *cf.* especially Ez. xxxiv.

The second " Massa " is strongly eschatological in tone. It opens with an attack on Jerusalem, which is repulsed through divine action. In xii, 9-14 we have an intriguing passage which speaks of various families, all plunged in mourning and keeping themselves apart from one another and the rest of Judah.

These are sometimes explained, like the preceding " Massa,"
as referring to events which took place in the Maccabaean age.

Ch. xiii, 1-6 offer us a picture of the purification which
Judah is to undergo. It is interesting to note that among the
evils to be eliminated, the prophets are included. Indeed, the
accusation of being a prophet is so serious that a man will
make the most absurd excuse to explain the scars of wounds
he has inflicted on himself in his ecstatic frenzy (xiii, 3-6).

It is widely held that xiii, 7-9, with the reference to " shepherds," has been misplaced, and should belong to the preceding " Massa." The position usually assigned to it is after
xi. 14.

The book concludes (ch. xiv) with a picture of the ideal
future. Jerusalem is to be the true spiritual centre of all the
people, and those who will not accept the supremacy of the
city and its cultus are to be destroyed. The city itself is to be
truly consecrated, and even the humblest vessels and ornaments
are to be stamped with holiness to Yahweh.

Malachi. As we have already noted, this third " Massa "
has attained the rank of a separate book, and a title has been
found for it. It consists almost entirely of poetic oracles, and
clearly belongs to the post-exilic period, probably to the earlier
part of it. The term used in i, 8 for " Governor " indicates
a Persian official rather than a Greek.

The prophet is greatly interested in the Temple ritual and
in the priesthood. Thus in i, 6-14 he insists that sacrificial
victims should be perfect animals; a human ruler would not
be satisfied with anything less than the best. Tithes must be
duly paid (iii, 7-12); to withhold them is robbing God. Priests
are condemned because they have not fulfilled their duties
properly (ii, 1-9). Incidentally we notice that priests are
identified with Levites, and that the stress is laid on their
judicial functions rather than on their position in the cultus,
suggesting again that the prophet belongs to a period even
earlier than that of Ezra.

" Malachi " speaks strongly against divorce. Though it was
familiar and permitted by law, this man feels strongly that it
is a breach of divine law. Few if any others in the ancient east
would have adopted such a position.

Another striking feature of this book is its universality.
There is none of that narrow Judaism which would subjugate
or destroy all other peoples. All genuine worship, he believes,

is offered to Yahweh, whether the worshippers realise it or not (i, 11, ii, 10).

Finally, there is a strong eschatological element in the teaching of this book. We are reminded that Yahweh will suddenly come to His Temple (iii, 1-3), and the ideal age will be ushered in. The book ends with the prediction of Elijah's return to prepare for the end of the age (iv, 4-6). Christian thought recognised that this prediction was fulfilled in John the Baptist, and it is significant that in our Bibles the last word of a prophet is the first in the Gospel story.

CHAPTER XV

THE WRITINGS : HEBREW POETIC FORM

WHENEVER we make a statement, or even produce a short series of sounds, it is easier for us to repeat it than to utter something quite fresh. This is true both of poetry and of prose, but in poetry the repetition is always more accurate than it is in prose. The way in which this " expectation " is roused and satisfied in poetic form varies a good deal. In the types which are familiar in Europe, it is always a sound or series of sounds. In Latin and Greek poetry, we have a number of syllables, some of which are long and others short, and they are arranged in a definite pattern which is repeated again and again, with certain permissible variations to avoid monotony. In most modern European poetic forms, it is the series of accented and unaccented syllables which go to make up the verse rhythm. In many forms of poetry we have the same sound at the end of consecutive or nearly consecutive lines; we call this " Rhyme."

In all these cases the verse form depends on sound. But in the oldest poetry known to us, the deciding factor was not sound but thought. The poet said something, and so raised a certain expectation in the minds of his hearers. Then he said it again in other words, or developed his theme in a way which recalled the first remark. Thus every line of Hebrew poetry has two parts, or sometimes three. Normally they are linked together by being more or less " parallel " to one another. Attempts have been made during the last fifty or sixty

I

years to find a sound rhythm as well as a thought rhythm in Hebrew poetry, but so far they have hardly been successful. Hebrew is a strongly accented language, and the rhythms of its sounds apply as much to prose as to poetry. But we seldom meet with regular " parallelism " in prose.

The shortest unit of Hebrew verse, which is sometimes called the " verse-member " and sometimes the " colon," must have at least two main ideas, and seldom if ever has more than three. These may be combined in various ways, and there are well-recognised forms of parallelism. For example, it may be complete, when every idea in one member corresponds to an idea in the next. So in Ps. xci, 5 we read :

> Thou-shalt-not-be-afraid for-the-terror by-night,
>   Nor-for-the-arrow that-flieth by-day;
> Nor-for-the-pestilence that-walketh in-darkness,
>   Nor-for-the-destruction that-wasteth at-noonday.

(Each group of hyphened words represents a single word or significant idea in Hebrew.)

Here are two lines, each in two parts. In the second line the two parts are exactly balanced; every idea in the first member has a corresponding idea in the second. We might put them this way :

> (Nor for the pestilence)   (that walketh)   (in darkness)
> (Nor for the destruction)   (that wasteth)   (at noonday)

We call this *complete parallelism.* But a whole poem written in this way would become unbearably monotonous, and it is not often that parallelism is so absolutely complete. More often it is *incomplete,* that is to say, only a part of the second member corresponds exactly to a part of the first member. Here again, we may have two types. In the first of the two verses quoted we have three " units " in each member. " Terror " and " by night " in the first member correspond to " arrow " and " by day " in the second, but there is nothing in the second to balance " Thou shalt not be afraid " in the first, and nothing in the first to balance " that flieth " in the second. This is called " Incomplete parallelism with compensation." Quite often, however, there is nothing in the second member corresponding to one of the first. So in Ps. cxxi, 6 we read :

> The sun shall not smite thee by day,
>   Nor the moon by night.

Here " sun " and " moon " correspond to one another, and so also " day " and " night," but there is nothing in the second member to balance " shall . . . smite." This is " Incomplete parallelism without compensation," and it generally means that the second member is shorter than the first.

Sometimes there is no discernible parallelism at all, and it seems that the sense runs straight on. But close examination will show that there is still some balance in the *number* of significant ideas, and elsewhere in the poem there is nearly always a clear parallelism of thought. This has been called " synthetic " or " formal " parallelism.

All this refers to parallelism between the two members of the same line. But we often find that one whole line is parallel to that which precedes or follows it. Thus in Ps. xxvii, 1 we have :

> The Lord is my light and my salvation;
> Whom shall I fear?
> The Lord is the strength of my life;
> Of whom shall I be afraid?

Here are two lines, containing four members. The first and third members are parallel to one another, and so also the second and fourth. In other words, it is the complete lines that are parallel, not the members within the line. This we call " external parallelism."

Every line, then, is made up of two parts, each of which contains either two or three significant words or ideas. Thus there may be different arrangements, and we often call these " metres," though the word does not mean exactly the same as it does when we are speaking of normal European verse. The names we give to them are simply the figures denoting the number of significant words in each part of the line. Thus the verse quoted from Ps. xci is 3 :3, that from cxxi is 3 :2, so also that from Ps. xxvii. Another form is 2 :2; we find it in Ps. xxix, 1 :

> Give unto the Lord,
> O ye sons of the mighty,
> Give unto the Lord
> Glory and strength.

Occasionally, too, we get a third member, either with two or with three significant words, so producing 2 :2 :2 or 3 :3 :3. As a rule we find these two only in poems whose prevailing " metre " is 3 :3. On the other hand we normally find both 3 :2 and 2 :2 in the same poem. Ps. xxiii is a good example. It is all 3 :2 except v. 4, which runs :

> Yea, though-I-walk
>> Through-the-valley of-the-shadow-of-death,
> I-will-fear-no evil;
>> For-thou-art with-me;
> Thy-rod and-thy-staff,
>> They comfort-me.

This gives us the main types of Hebrew verse-form. Occasionally we have 3 : 3 : 3, *e.g.* in Ps. c, and there is a rare form sometimes described as 4 : 3, though it is really 2 : 2 : 3. A good example occurs in Jeremiah iv, 23-26; vv. 23*f.* run :

>> I-beheld the-earth,
>>> And-lo, it-was-without-form-and-void;
>>>> And-the-heavens, and-they-had-no light.
>> I-beheld the-mountains,
>>> And-lo, they-trembled,
>>>> And-all the-hills moved-lightly.

But we very rarely find a 3 : 3 in the middle of 3 : 2 or 2 : 2, or one of these shorter forms in the middle of 3 : 3. When we do come across them, we are inclined to suspect that there has been a mistake in copying the poem at some point in the history of its transmission. This impression is often confirmed by other ovidence.

In some poems we find groups of lines which clearly form " stanzas." It does not follow that we can divide all Hebrew poems into these regular "verse-paragraphs," but this is a form which must certainly be taken into account. There are one or two indications which make it certain that such an arrangement was intentional.

There are Psalms in which we have a " refrain " at regular intervals. Ps. xlvi is a good example. Here we have three " stanzas," each containing six 2 : 2 lines. These are vv. 1-3, 4-6, and 8-10. In vv. 7 and 11 we have the same refrain :

> The-Lord of-hosts is-with-us;
> The-God of-Jacob is-our-refuge.

It seems fairly clear that this has accidentally been left out after v.3, and it is to be noted that the " metre " of the refrain is 3 : 3. Some of us suspect that it was added long after the original hymn was composed; the metre is not the only indication which points to an addition. Still, the stanza form is there; the refrain merely emphasises it.

Another ingenious arrangement which we find in some Hebrew poems is the " acrostic." We often find this as a kind of puzzle in English. A word or a sentence begins with a particular letter, and these initial letters can be read as a word or a sentence. The Hebrew acrostic is always alphabetical. Each line or group of lines begins with a new letter, and they are placed in the proper order. An older generation used to learn its English alphabet from a " poem " which began :

> " A was an Archer, and shot at a frog,
> B was a Butcher, and had a large dog."

This was an " alphabetic acrostic," and we have several poems which are ingeniously constructed on this principle in Hebrew. The most elaborate is Ps. cxix, where we have the poem divided into twenty-two groups (there are twenty-two letters in the Hebrew alphabet) and each line in the group begins with the same letter. In some Bibles the Hebrew letter itself is printed at the head of each group. There is no other case in our Bibles where so many lines are given to each letter; usually there is only one, or at most two, but there are three poems in the Book of Lamentations where each letter has three lines. In two of these poems, however, it is only the first of the three lines which carries the acrostic letter, and this is the usual arrangement also where there are two lines, as in Ps. xxxvii.

In poems constructed like this we may be fairly sure that some kind of stanza arrangement was intended. But it is by no means universal, though some scholars have attempted to divide all the Psalms into stanzas of this sort. Some think that the mysterious word " Selah " meant that a stanza had ended and a refrain was to be sung. There are Psalms (e.g. xlvi) which seem to bear out this theory, but in a large number of others it does not fit. We must be content to regard the stanza arrangement as possible and occasional, but by no means universal in Hebrew poetry. What must be regarded as universal is the parallelism, of one kind or another; if there is no parallelism the passage is prose, not poetry.

CHAPTER XVI

THE WRITINGS : THE PSALMS

THE Book of Psalms as it has come down to us is the hymn-book of the second Temple. But it undoubtedly contains pieces which are centuries older than this Temple, though the older hymns may have undergone some modification in the course of centuries. From time to time men alter or add to their hymns, as their spiritual experience grows and needs expression. Many of our best-known Christian hymns have been thus altered, and we have direct evidence of changes made in some of the Psalms.

The Psalter is now divided into five "books," in imitation of the five books of the Pentateuch. They are : i-xli, xlii-lxxii, lxxiii-lxxxix, xc-cvi, cvii-cl. But it is clear that the collection includes poems taken from several earlier hymn-books. The most striking instance is to be seen in the second and third of the present "books," Pss. xlii-lxxxix. It is a curious fact that, except in the last six of these, the divine name Yahweh is comparatively rare, whereas it is the normal word for the God of Israel in all other parts of the Psalter. There are grounds for believing that this was often due to a deliberate change. It is difficult to see why a writer should have avoided the name Yahweh so completely in his composition. Sometimes we meet with phrases like "O God, my God" (Ps. xliii, 4), which would more naturally have run "Yahweh, my God." And in one or two cases we have the same Psalm, or part of a Psalm, in more than one place. Thus it seems certain that Pss. xiv and liii are variant forms of the same Psalm, with some alteration in vv. 5f. The name Yahweh occurs four times in Ps. xiv, and nowhere in liii; except in v. 6 it is replaced by the common term God. It is difficult to avoid the conclusion that the greater part of this middle third of the book once formed a collection commonly called "Elohistic" made by people who had reasons for avoiding the use of the divine name, probably for fear that it might be profaned. Pss. lxxxiv-lxxxix, which use the name Yahweh freely, may have been added when the collection was included in the present Psalter.

Then, too, most Psalms have headings or "titles"; in the Hebrew Bible these are often counted as the first verse of the Psalm. Some of these appear to be musical directions, or descriptions of special kinds of Psalm. But there are also personal names, David, Asaph, Sons of Korah, Ethan, Solomon, Moses. In each case the name is introduced by a preposition, which may mean "to," "for," "of," or "according to." In the English Bible it is rendered "of" where it appears before a proper name (in Ps. lxxii A.V. has "for," R.V.

" of "), but as " to " when it is placed before the term translated " Chief Musician." Tradition has taken this preposition
to imply authorship, and this may be the correct explanation,
but it is by no means certain that it is.

It is significant that the names tend to occur in groups. The
only name in Bk. I is that of David, and this is absent only
from Pss. i, ii, x, and xxxiii. Is it too much to suggest that
Bk. I originally formed a collection by itself, consisting almost
entirely of Psalms bearing the name of David? The same
name occurs in later Psalms. Some of these are isolated, but
twice we have distinct groups, li-lxx (except lxvi, lxvii) and
cxxxviii-cxlv. We have, too, that curious note at the end of
Ps. lxxii : " The prayers of David, the son of Jesse, are
ended." May there not have been a second Davidic collection,
known as " The Prayers of David?"

The Korah Psalms are mainly in one group, xlii-xlix (Ps.
xliii is really the last stanza of Ps. xlii, and has been
accidentally divided from it). There is a second group of four,
Pss. lxxxiv-lxxxviii (Ps. lxxxvi is an exception here). It seems
as though the earlier group had been included in the Elohistic
collection, and the other four had been omitted.

One Asaph Psalm (Ps. 1) stands alone; the other eleven
are all together, Pss. lxxiii-lxxxiii. The other names occur once
only in each case.

Up to the end of the nineteenth century, scholars were much
concerned with questions of the date and authorship of the
Psalms. It seems, however, that no certain conclusions are
generally possible. In some cases we have points of vocabulary
and grammar which suggest a comparatively late or comparatively early date. But the value of the Psalms is not
dependent on their date, or on their authorship, but on the
place they take in the human experience of God.

During the last fifty years, interest has shifted to the actual
use of the Psalms. It is assumed that every one had a definite
place in the worship of Israel. Some were intended for national
occasions, and others for private and personal forms of
worship. It has been observed that certain forms are suited to
special purposes and types of service. Thus, for example, a
hymn of praise or of thanksgiving will normally begin with a
call to praise, followed by the reasons for which the worshipper feels impelled to the particular act of worship. Ps. ciii
is a good example; it begins with two verses in which the

speaker calls on himself to " bless " Yahweh. The next three
verses are a summary of the benefits which he himself has
received, and the greater part of the Psalm is devoted to a
description of the goodness of Yahweh to all who are faithful
to Him. It ends with a general call to all Yahweh's servants
and creatures to join in the universal chorus of blessing.

The following are the main classes generally recognised :

1.   Songs of praise.
2.   National Laments.
3.   Royal Psalms.
4.   Individual Laments.
5.   Individual Thanksgivings.

There are half a dozen smaller classes, including special
subjects like praise of the Law, or meditation on the great
problems of life. Pss. xix and cxix illustrate the first class and
Ps. lxxiii the second. We have also a special group in Pss.
cxx-cxxxiv. These are called in the A.V. " Songs of Degrees,"
and in the R.V. " Songs of Ascents." They seem to belong to
different classes, but have been assembled for a particular
purpose, probably for use by travellers on pilgrimage to
Jerusalem. We generally now call them " Pilgrim Psalms."

The first class includes several types. One of the most
striking is that of the " enthronement " Psalms, which show
Yahweh as a king ascending his throne. Some scholars hold
that there was a festival every year in pre-exilic days at which
Yahweh was held to resume his authority as King of the
world, and His accession was hailed by the worshippers with
the cry " Yahweh is King!" Psalms xciii, xcvii and xcix
begin in this way, and the whole group in which they are
included would be suitable for such a purpose. These are not
to be confused with the " Royal " Psalms, which celebrate a
human king, and are also to be ascribed to the period of the
monarchy. Thus in Ps. xviii we have a song of victory,
ascribed to David and now also found in II Sam. xxii. Ps. xlv
is an ode on the marriage of a king, and Ps. lxxii is a prayer
for a king on his accession.

" Laments of the Nation " are the kind of hymn which
would be sung at times of depression, disaster, or danger. We
have striking examples in Pss. xliv and lxxiv, and it is to be
noted that the Psalmist often goes back to the record of
marvels wrought by Yahweh in delivering His people, and
an appeal to Him to repeat His mighty deeds. They would be

well suited to such an occasion as a public fast proclaimed in face of national peril. The worshippers sometimes declare their innocence; they have not deserved this treatment, and cannot understand it. But they believe that Yahweh has brought suffering upon them, and He can remove it.

Perhaps the largest class of all is that of the " Individual Laments." It must be remembered that congregational worship was not native to the Temple; it was, in fact, developed in the Synagogue, and certainly does not go back beyond the exile. There were, of course, great occasions when sacrifice was offered for the whole people, and large numbers were gathered to witness it, but this is not congregational worship as we understand it, where every individual has some part to play, vocal or silent. But the Temple was the centre of life for all Israel. It was even the final court of justice; where a case could not be settled by local or other secular officials, Yahweh must decide it, and He gave His verdict in the sanctuary through the priests. Many of these " Individual Laments " are protestations of innocence; Ps. xxvi, for example, begins with the words, " Judge me, O Yahweh, for I have walked in mine integrity." At times we find a curse invoked on the " adversary," i.e. the accuser. This is not merely vindictive passion. The accuser has sent out a curse into the world, a living and vigorous thing which will be a deadly peril to the person whom it strikes. It must strike somewhere, and, since the accused protests his innocence, on whom could it fall more properly than on the man who let it loose without good cause?

There are times when the accused admits his sin, and pleads for forgiveness. The Church has long recognised a group of " Penitential " Psalms (vi, xxxii, xxxviii, li, cii, cxxx, cxlii). Some of these and similar Psalms suggest a short liturgy. In Ps. vi, for example, the actual prayer goes down to v. 7. We may suppose that this was followed by an interval in which the case was considered and decided, and when judgment was given in the defendant's favour he would break out into vv. 8-10 : " Depart from me, all ye workers of iniquity; for Yahweh hath heard the voice of my weeping. . . ." We note a similar change in Ps. xxviii, where vv. 1-5 belong to the first part and vv. 6-9 to the second part of the proceedings. It is to be noted that Psalms of this type do not contain any specific statement of the accusation or of the sin; they are suited to any particular set of circumstances within the general range to which they apply. This is what we should expect from a liturgical form to be used in a number of cases belonging to the same broad class.

"Individual Thanksgivings" also seem to have been adapted for use in some form of liturgy. Some of them clearly refer to the performance of vows. Thus in Ps. lxvi, 13 the Psalmist says he has come to the Temple to bring burnt-offerings in fulfilment of his vows. We have clearer indications of liturgical form in Ps. cxvi, where, in v. 12, the worshipper asks the ritual question, " What shall I render . . ." and on receiving the priest's reply, continues, " I will pay my vows . . ." There are Psalms which naturally attach themselves to this group, though they are not cast in any special form, or adapted to any particular ritual. Some appear to be quite independent of any form of ritual, and to be simply personal meditations. These include some of the best known and best loved; we could ill have dispensed with Pss. xxiii and lxxiii. The one is the most perfect expression of quiet trust in God that we know, and the other tells of an inward struggle, brought about by one of the most terrible among religious problems, the question of undeserved suffering.

All this is but concerned with the outward form of the book and the Psalms in it. It is impossible to give any comprehensive account of the teaching and the value of the Psalms for us today. Each must be treated individually from this point of view, for they cover practically the whole range of spiritual experience. It is not an accident that not only the Jewish people but also the Christian Church has known and treasured these monuments of piety through the centuries. Even today they play no small part in Christian worship. They vary greatly in literary quality, but we hardly notice the differences between them as we sing or read them. They are filled with the experience of the ages, and carry far more than their mere words or form can convey. Generation after generation has read into them its own conditions and its own faith. There are expressions and thoughts in the book which have been discarded with a growing knowledge of God; no Christian can approve the sentiment with which Ps. cxxxvii ends—but how human it is! It seems as if we had almost every aspect of man's relation to God depicted in these poems, simple and happy trust, the sense of sin, the appeal to a higher power in trouble of every kind, and the conviction that the whole world, physical and human, is in the hand of a loving and righteous God who seeks always the best for his children. The Psalter has entered so deeply into the human heart that it will remain a great treasury of spiritual life and direction as long as man needs God.

CHAPTER XVII

THE WRITINGS : JOB

THE greatest problem man has had to face is that of suffering. It has a practical side; how can we get rid of it? The only complete solution ever offered is that of Buddhism, which recognises that pain is a universal element in human experience, and that it can be ended only with the extinction of individual personality. But people like the Hebrews clung to their personality at all costs. It was worth all the suffering that can be inflicted if they could be and remain persons. They believed in a personal God, and as they came to recognise His perfect justice and His omnipotence, they began to ask questions. In other words, their problem was not merely a practical task to be performed, it was a question which struck at the roots of their spiritual life.

A problem of this kind is produced by the conflict between a theory and a fact. The theory was that all events were governed and controlled—even planned—by an omnipotent and perfectly righteous God. The prophets had insisted that sin would always produce suffering; to that extent the problem was easily solved. But there was so much suffering which could not by any possibility be traced to sin, even the sin of the community to which the sufferer belonged. Here was the fact, and it seemed wholly incompatible with the theory.

The problem could not have arisen outside Israel, but when once the teaching of the great prophets had taken firm hold on the people, its emergence was inevitable. Some of the more serious thinkers in Israel devoted time and thought to it. The great prophet to whom we owe the picture of the Suffering Servant held that the pain of the perfect man might be redemptive, even vicarious, and that he would be satisfied by the knowledge that he had thus won peace and forgiveness for others. This was enough from the sufferer's point of view, but did it justify God? The poet responsible for Ps. lxxiii had been tempted to discard his theory and abandon his belief in goodness; later his danger was that of rejoicing over the punishment of the wicked. But the most thorough treatment of the whole subject is to be found in the book of Job.

That book offers us a poem which may well claim a place among the greatest pieces of the world's literature. It has a high theme, its language is lofty and inspiring, it is marked by a fearless sincerity, its author has a grim sense of humour, sketches his characters brilliantly, and shows great skill in weaving them into his plan of thought. It defies any attempt at classification, for it is not an epic or a drama, unless these terms can apply to a poem in which there is no physical action at all, though there is progress of thought and high emotional tension. It might be called a philosophical dialogue, but it is far more than this; it is the autobiography of a soul battling against despair. Perhaps Dante is the only European poet who can be compared with this writer, and even Dante falls far below him.

It is difficult to believe that the book as a whole is the work of a single author. At the beginning and the end we have a story of a man who suffered through the schemes of the Satan, and in the end triumphed over the Adversary, and over his friends. This is in prose, and looks like a popular tale. It differs in several ways from the poem to which it forms an introduction and a conclusion; the divine name Yahweh is normal in the prose and very rare in the poem. Job's attitude and character is hardly consistent in the two parts. In the conclusion of the prose story Job receives divine approval, in the poem he is condemned by God. But, above all, there is a complete difference of outlook. The prose story tells the tale of the sufferer from the outside; the writer is a spectator, sympathetic, perhaps, but still a spectator. The Job of the poem is the poet himself; it is his own experience that he describes with passion and with hope. He has written it with his own heart's blood.

There are sections in the poem itself which many scholars regard as later additions. Ch. xxviii, for example, is a hymn in praise of wisdom which plays no part in the development of the theme. In chs. xxxii-xxxvii we have speeches by Elihu, a character who has not been previously mentioned. He adds nothing to the discussion, and no further reference is made to him, while his style, though lofty and impressive, hardly reaches the level attained elsewhere in the poem. Doubts have also been cast on the originality of xl. 15-xli, 34, where two monstrous creatures, the hippopotamus and the crocodile, are described. They might be omitted without serious loss to the poem, but the reasons against their originality are by no means so strong as those which have led scholars to eliminate the other sections mentioned from the original book.

Three solutions (if that be the right term) to the problem of suffering are offered in the book. The first is that of the popular tale, whose beginning and end alone have survived. Here we are taken into the Council of Yahweh. In His presence His servants are gathered to report on their activities. Among them is one whose function it is to see that men really are righteous, and, if he suspects them, to summon them to trial by Yahweh. Yahweh mentions Job, the perfect man whose life has been spent in honour and prosperity; is he what he seems to be? The Satan replies that this question cannot be answered till Job has been tested, and gets permission to reduce him to abject poverty. In a few minutes Job hears that all his property has been stolen or destroyed, and that all his children have been killed. He stands this test, but, in a further interview with Yahweh, the Satan is given permission to touch the man himself. He does so, and Job is smitten with terrible boils (in the poem the symptoms make it clear that the disease assumed there is a virulent form of leprosy). Job still maintains his attitude of humble and pious submission, and three friends, Eliphaz, Bildad, and Zophar, come to condole with him.

At this point the poet enters, and a debate between the four men begins. There are three stages, in each one Eliphaz, Bildad and Zophar speak once, and Job answers them one by one. As our text stands, Bildad's speech in the third round is very short and Zophar is silent. There is, however, an impression among scholars that this is due to accidental omission and slight alteration of the text. Commentators are inclined to ascribe ch. xxvi to Bildad, not to Job, and to suggest that between xxvii, 6 and 7 the end of Job's speech and the beginning of Zophar's have dropped out. Certainly xxvii, 7-23 sound far more like one of the friends than Job.

The friends represent the conventional theology of the

poet's time. They have only one thing to say, and they repeat it with increasing emphasis and growing heat. They start from the truth that all sin results in suffering. From this they conclude that all suffering is the result of sin. We may condemn their logic, but they are not the first or the last to stumble into this fallacy. Job has suffered, therefore he has sinned. Let him confess, humble himself before God, and doubtless he will receive pardon and restoration.

That is all the friends have to say, and they say it eight or nine times over. But there are two points of interest in them. In the first place, they are clearly differentiated from one another. All are good men, devout and kindly, anxious to give all the help they can to their suffering friend. But their characters are very different. Eliphaz is the mystic, who has had special experiences of the presence and teaching of God. Bildad is the scholar; he knows all that the wise have said in ages gone by. Zophar is the pure dogmatist and appeals neither to revelation nor to history. He knows, and can speak with authority of what God wills for men.

The second point of interest lies in the fact that, while their position does not change and Job moves steadily onwards, most of his steps in advance are based on something the friends have said. Job's first speech is simply a cry of pain, and longing for death which alone can deliver him. Eliphaz, with tender courtesy, states the orthodox view, and promises Job that all may yet be well with him. Neither Euripides nor G. B. Shaw ever exposed the futility of a conventional orthodoxy so ruthlessly as the poet does here. Job *knows* that he has not sinned in such fashion as to deserve this punishment. He *knows* that nothing can restore his dead children. He *knows* that he is suffering from an incurable disease, and that death is the only prospect before him. What is the use of these smooth platitudes, however kind be the thought behind them, and however saintly be the man who utters them?

Yet Eliphaz has said something of importance. After all, it is God who has brought disaster upon Job. Is God, then, his enemy? This is a new thought, even more terrible than any of the blows that have fallen on Job, and it is hardly mitigated by the conviction that, when it is too late, God will realise His mistake, and look for Job in vain.

Bildad then states his view. In essence it is that of Eliphaz, but he lays stress on the righteousness of God. Now that term has two meanings not always easy to distinguish. It was originally used in law and applied to the person who won his case. Gradually it acquired the sense of the person who ought to win his case, and so gained a moral quality, though it never quite lost its legal significance. It is this on which Job's mind fastens. He begins to think of his relation to God in terms of a lawsuit; he has a case to present, and he firmly believes that he is in the right. But that will not help him. God, the all-powerful, is bound to win the case. He is " righteous " in that sense, because no one can stand against Him. The thought only makes Job more desperate, but he cannot get it out of his head, and henceforward it dominates his mind.

Zophar speaks. He, too, has nothing to add to what Eliphaz has said, but we feel the growing irritation produced by Job's obstinate refusal to accept the friends' advice, confess that he is a sinner, and humble himself before God. But he does make one fruitful remark; it is useless to bring a lawsuit against God, for He cannot be found unless He chooses to reveal Himself : " Canst thou by searching find out God?" he asks (xi, 7). Here is a new difficulty for Job; he tries to ignore it, but it forces its way to the front at times and he cries " Why hidest Thou Thy face?" (xiii, 24). He has no time for his quest, for death is before him. A tree may sprout afresh when it has been cut down, but there is no such hope for man. Here is a germ which is to spring up and bear fruit later, but now it only adds to the gloom.

The second speech of Eliphaz repeats the old doctrine, with rather more emphasis on Job's sinfulness. But Job will not abandon his position. He insists on believing in two apparently contradictory statements; God is tormenting him unjustly, and God is essentially just. At last he makes a great leap of faith and claims the right of appeal. To whom can he appeal? Only to God, God as He really must be and not God as the friends represent Him (xvi, 18-21). But at once he falls back into a yet lower depth; he must die before his appeal can be heard.

After Bildad's second speech the emotional tension reaches its height. In the most impassioned utterance in the whole book Job at length makes a further leap. God being what He is, He cannot allow death to end all relations between Himself and His worshippers. " I know," he cries, " that my champion lives, and shall stand on the earth hereafter;

(the first half of xix, 26 is unintelligible, but Job goes on :)
> ... and apart from my flesh I shall see God,
>> Whom I shall behold for myself, my eyes shall see Him,
>> and not another's;
>>> Though my reins have perished in my bosom.

So the great passage xix, 25-27. Even the total dissolution of his physical frame will not end the matter; somehow and somewhere Job will find God for himself. This is not strictly a doctrine of immortality in the sense of being eternal life. That might come later, but for the present it is enough for Job to know that even death is not the end. At last he has found solid ground on which to stand. His problems are not solved, his questions are not answered, but at least he is sure of God, and will accept whatever may be given to him.

From this point onwards the friends are comparatively unimportant except in so far as they provide a foil for Job. In his next speech (ch. xxi) he states the whole great problem clearly and almost calmly. He still wishes to meet with God, and sometimes the desire for the opportunity to present his case overcomes him with a sense of the hopelessness of the search for God (cf. xxiii, 3). But, when the friends have said all they have to say, Job utters his final challenge and presents his case. His final speech in the debate occupies chs. xxix-xxxi, and in the last of these he takes a magnificent oath of purgation, asserting his innocence and the purity of his life. This chapter has been described as the highest statement of an ethical code which the Old Testament contains, and it is not till we come to the New Testament that we can find a parallel to it.

At last, in ch. xxxviii, God appears and speaks. But there is not a single word about Job's problem. Instead God calls attention to His own might and power, and Job falls in utter humility before Him confessing that he has been wrong, though he has realised his actual position only when he has been in the very presence of God.

The poet thus does not offer us an intellectual solution of the great problem. Possibly the human mind, being finite, never will attain a complete answer. The western temperament lacks that intense reverence for power which seems to dominate the east, and is less likely to be satisfied, as Job was, with the exhibition of divine greatness. But this is a detail which belongs to the age and the race of the poet. The essential fact is that in the presence of God the problem has ceased to trouble him. In the glory of that vision all meaner and lesser things have faded into insignificance. The intellectual problem may remain unsolved, but the deeper spirit is satisfied. He who has really seen God as He is, needs no further answer to his questions.

CHAPTER XVIII

THE WRITINGS : PROVERBS

THE ultimate aim of all philosophy is the unification of experience, the discovery of basic principles which may be manifested in a number of different ways. Natural science attempts to do this for the physical world; it finds that such diverse phenomena as the fall of an apple from a tree and the movement of the tides can be explained as examples of the same principle, which it calls the law of gravitation. In ethics we seek to reduce right human conduct to a certain number of moral principles, love, service, self-denial, and others; we believe that by applying these to every situation we can achieve the good life. In metaphysics we try to take into account not only the physical and the ethical, but also the very nature of being, and embark on the quest of ultimate reality.

It is sometimes said that the Hebrew mind was incapable of philosophic thinking. If this simply means that the Old Testament does not present us with an organised metaphysical theory, it is justified, but that is only the most developed form of philosophy, and we can find its simpler types in the speech and thought in many places here and elsewhere. The most elementary thinker makes some attempt at generalising his experience, though he may not go far in the search for a common principle. When the " unlettered hind " says :

> A rainbow at night
> Is the shepherd's delight;
> A rainbow in the morning
> Is the shepherd's warning.

he is summarising his experience of certain kinds of weather. His judgment is based solely on observations made by himself and others, but it is confirmed and " explained " by

K

meteorological science. This is philosophy, embryonic perhaps, but still philosophy.

There is, therefore, a widely spread tendency to sum up experience in short, pithy sayings. To these, among other forms of organised speech, the Hebrew gave the name " Mashal," which we commonly render as " Proverbs." The Hebrews were not alone in making collections of these; such volumes of generalisations appear as far apart as Greece and India, while interesting collections are found also in the literature of Mesopotamia and of Egypt.

For readers of the Old Testament, the great body of such epigrammatic generalisations is to be found in the Book of Proverbs. Tradition held that the great author was Solomon, who had a reputation for " wisdom," and his name has naturally been prefixed to this book. It is, however, a collection of collections, and not all are ascribed to Solomon. The groups are :

1. Chs. i-ix. Proverbs of Solomon (but perhaps the first seven verses belong to the whole book and not to this collection).
2. Chs. x, 1-xxii, 16. Proverbs of Solomon.
3. Chs. xxii, 17-xxiv, 22. "Words of the Wise."
4. Ch. xxiv, 23-34. Further words of the Wise.
5. Chs. xxv-xxix. Proverbs of Solomon, collected by the men of Hezekiah.
6. Ch. xxx. Words of Agur.
7. Ch. xxxi, 1-9. Words of Lemuel.
8. Ch. xxxi, 10-31. An alphabetic acrostic poem on the virtuous woman.

The first of these sections stands out as distinct from the rest. The others, except for the last, are real collections of " wise " sayings; this chapter gives much more direct instruction to youth. After the introduction (i, 1-7) the speaker at once assumes the role of a father, or, it may be, a teacher, and we have a series of connected discourses. Sometimes the teacher is Wisdom herself personified, giving good advice to young men. They are especially warned against the wiles of the immoral woman, and one long section (vii, 5-23) is given to an account of the way in which a married woman seduces a guileless youth.

The most striking feature of this division, however, is to be seen in the relation of Wisdom to Yahweh. She is in places fully personified, and in viii 22ff she is described as the oldest of all that God has made. At the same time she is still an element in the divine being, and we have an adumbration of a thought which finds its most complete expression in the Christian doctrine of the Trinity.

In the main, the advice given in **Proverbs** is sound. The character of the fool is often held up as a warning, and it is clear that the term has a strong ethical content; it is not merely a person who is intellectually stupid. At the same time such a man must be lacking in brains, or he would see that it is to his worldly advantage to behave himself properly. Folly has many forms; we have pictures of the lazy, the impious, the unfilial, the conceited, and many another reprehensible type. Advice is given as to the best methods of dealing with such people, though it is not always easy to see the best method. In xxvi, 4 and 5, for example, we have a direct contradiction; the former verse bids us refrain from answering a fool, the latter advises us to do so. A good reason is given in both cases, and we are left to choose for ourselves.

We have interesting pictures of social life. The sense of the family is strong, and a number of proverbs deal with the attitude of children to their parents and the right treatment of children. Women are sometimes mentioned, but it is curious to note that they are seldom if ever directly addressed. We suspect sometimes that the proverb-maker had a Xanthippe in his household. On the other hand, the value of a good wife is strongly emphasised, and, as we have seen, the book ends with a panegyric on the virtuous wife. At times kings appear, and it is clear that their position is that of the absolute autocrat, who must be rightly treated. He, however, has to recognise that he is subordinate to Yahweh, even though he can do as he will with his own subjects. In dealing with his fellows a man should cultivate honesty and self-control. Veracity is warmly commended, especially in legal matters; every one who has any experience of the east knows how difficult it is to be sure that a witness is reliable.

All through we get the feeling that the motives for right conduct are not the highest. Goodness pays, honesty is the best policy; these are the controlling incentives presented normally in the proverbs, and we miss the moral passion which is so prominent in the great prophets. It is seldom that we have an appeal to ultimate ethical standards; Old Testament religion does not reach its climax in **Proverbs.**

This does not mean that there is no appeal to religion. On the contrary, there are numbers of references to the reaction of Yahweh to human conduct. Men are warned that He will reward the righteous and punish the wicked, in accordance with the principles which have long been recognised. Even sacrifice must be offered with a pure spirit, and not to cloak iniquity. At the same time, the motive here also is prudential. It is hope or fear of consequences which impels men to live an upright life and eschew iniquity. We miss that search for God, that delight in His presence which is often prominent in the Psalms, nor do we feel that the writers have been in the very Council of God as the prophets were. What is important from the proverb-maker's point of view is that man should keep on the right side of God. This may not be the highest form of religious feeling, but it does at least recognise the sovereignty of God, and, if consistently followed out, may well lead to a deeper appreciation of the divine personality.

It remains to notice some interesting links between our Book of Proverbs and similar literature emanating from other parts of the ancient world. As we have already noted, such collections are commonly found in many parts of the world. Some scholars, for example, have found links between the Hebrew work and that of the Greek sage Theognis. It is, however, doubtful whether any real contact can be established. From Mesopotamia we have the wisdom of Ahikar, which was widely known as part of an ancient story, and found a place at least in certain Jewish quarters, for an Aramaic translation was discovered among the documents unearthed in the old Jewish settlement at Elephantine, a southern outpost of Egypt. Here again there are resemblances rather than proof of direct borrowing. In Egypt itself, however, we have a document which contains points of resemblance too close to have been due to accidental causes. This is the so-called " Teaching of Amen-emope," embodying the words of a sage who is generally dated about 800 B.C. Here we find a close parallel with the third of the collections in our Book of Proverbs, chs. xxii, 17-xxiv, 22. The resemblance does not extend beyond Prov. xxiii, 12, but up to that point there are only three verses (xxii, 23, 26, 27) which have no parallel in the Egyptian document. It is difficult to escape the conclusion that there is a direct contact here. We cannot date individual proverbs, or even the main collections, so we cannot say for certain which is the original and which is the borrower. On *à priori* grounds the probability would seem to be that the Hebrew copied the Egyptian; it does not appear likely that a scholar in the ancient and cultured realm of Egypt would apply for wisdom to a younger and comparatively barbarous people. At the same time we must not exclude the possibility that even before the end of the ninth century this collection of " Words of the Wise " had become known in Egypt, and that some scholar had thought it worth his while to adopt certain of its precepts for the use of his own people. " Wisdom " was international, as science is today, and there is no overwhelming objection to the view that it was the Egyptian who relied on the philosophy of his northern neighbour.

CHAPTER XIX

THE WRITINGS: THE FIVE ROLLS

THIS is the name given to five short books which do not come under the heading of prophecy. Here we have poetry, " wisdom," and history, but it seems probable that the two books belonging to the latter class were written too late to be included in the list of the " Former Prophets," or were not recognised as worthy of a place in the Bible until that Canon was closed. The books, in the order given by the latest edition of the Hebrew Bible are: Ruth, The Song of Songs, Ecclesiastes, Lamentations, and Esther. We will glance at them one by one.

Ruth. Here we have a story coming from the age of the Judges. It does not claim to be contemporary with the events it describes, and, indeed, it expressly states that one incident belongs to the customs of former days, implying that it was no longer intelligible in the author's time (iv, 7). Here a bargain is ratified by drawing off a shoe. The explanation given here is far from being that of Deut. xxv. 5-10, where it is a permanent reproach to a man who has refused to do his duty to a dead kinsman.

The story is one of the most familiar in the Old Testament.

K*

It is beautifully told, and has a charm which has captured the imagination of countless artists and poets. An Israelite family, father, mother, and two sons, emigrates temporarily to Moab because of famine in the area of Bethlehem, their ancestral home. The sons marry, but die childless, following their father to the grave. The mother, Naomi, decides to return to Bethlehem, and Ruth, one of her daughters-in-law, insists on coming with her. They return at the beginning of the barley harvest (end of March or beginning of April), and Ruth goes out, as poor peasant women did, to glean behind the reapers. She happens to work in a piece of land farmed by Boaz, a relative of Naomi's dead husband. He is exceptionally kind to her, and Naomi tells her that, as a close relative, he has certain legal responsibilities to the dead and their living representatives. When all the harvest is over, Ruth, on Naomi's advice, goes to Boaz by night, and persuades him to carry out these legal obligations, which include the re-purchase of land sold by Naomi's husband, and the duty of marrying the childless widow, in order that the dead man's family may not be extinguished. There is one obstacle; Ruth's husband has left in Bethlehem a relative who stands nearer to him than Boaz does, and unless he refuses to act, Boaz himself has no standing. But the unnamed kinsman cannot face the prospect of begetting children for another man and not for himself, and Boaz undertakes the duties. A son is born to him, and the book closes with a short genealogy, showing that this son is David's grandfather.

The purpose of the book, as it seems, is to lay emphasis on the fact that David had Moabite blood in him. It has, then, been suggested that it was written in a period when marriage with a foreign woman was strongly condemned. The age of Nehemiah and Ezra comes naturally to mind, and the common explanation of the book is that it is a protest against the rigorous application of the principle imposed by both these reformers. It is clearly a comparatively late book, and, in addition to what has already been said, it may be noted that the writer does not seem to understand the old law of " levirate'' marriage. Certainly, as it appears in Deuteronomy xxv, it does not suggest that the brother-in-law may not have another wife, from whom he may get children who will carry on his family and name. Obviously, monogamy had become the rule by the writer's time, as it was not when the law was formulated. The latter part of the fourth century is as early as we can place it.

Song of Songs. Here we have a book which found its way into the Canon of Scripture only with great difficulty, and probably succeeded on the ground that it could be ascribed to Solomon. It contains a series of erotic lyrics, some of extra-ordinary freshness and beauty, and some, apparently, mutilated before they were included in the book. The language presents certain peculiarities; it is either late or cast in a northern dialect. But the interest of scholars has always lain in its interpretation rather than in its date or authorship.

Jewish and Christian theologians alike have found it diffi-cult to accept as canonical a book which, on the surface, deals with romantic human love. The problem was solved by taking it allegorically; Jews explained it as depicting the love of Yahweh for Israel, and Christians as a figure of the love existing between Christ and the Church. Each found justifica-tion for this view in other writings, both in the Old and in the New Testament.

Nineteenth-century scholars, however, saw in it a drama. Solomon, on progress through his northern dominions, was captivated by the beauty of a peasant girl, carried her off to his harem in Jerusalem, and eventually won her love. Another version introduced a third character, a rustic lover to whom the girl was faithful in spite of the king's wooing. Eventually he sent her back, and she rejoined her old lover.

There is, however, no ground for supposing that a secular drama ever existed in ancient Israel, or indeed, elsewhere in the ancient east. Religious drama was found as a part of special ritual, and may have been known in pre-exilic Israel, but even that has left only the faintest traces—if, indeed, it actually existed.

Modern Syrian practice has suggested to some scholars that in this book we have a reminiscence of a marriage ceremony. For a week the bridegroom and the bride are king and queen, and day after day various acts are performed and appropriate songs sung. On this theory Solomon would simply be the name chosen as that of the most glorious king of whom tradition knew. The bride is called a Shulamite, *i.e.* a " Solo-moness " (in any case this is the more probable meaning of the term).

It has also been suggested that this is a form of ritual belonging to the worship of the Mesopotamian Ishtar (Phoenician Astarte). The theory notes some interesting parallels, but before such a work would be included in the Scriptures, its origin must have been forgotten, and numerous changes made.

But, whatever the general interpretation may be, there can be no doubt that we have here a small collection of extremely beautiful lyrics. They have a freshness and delight in simple things which has few parallels and no superiors in the world's literature. We have the picture of a love-sick girl's dreams, the joy in nature as it shows itself in spring, the delight of the lover in his beloved's beauty, and his willingness to give up all else that men might desire for her. Nor can we regret its inclusion in the canon of Scripture. For the richest and most glorious of human experiences need for their full attainment the consciousness that they are linked with God.

Ecclesiastes. Like the Song of Songs, this book was admitted to the Jewish canon of Scripture only with difficulty, and on the ground that a tradition ascribed it to Solomon. In its present form, however, it cannot have been early, for the language in which it is written belongs to a later stage of Hebrew than that of the other books in the Old Testament, and resembles that commonly used in post-Biblical Rabbinic literature. Some scholars also feel that an original book has been modified and expanded by a later writer, who found the opinions expressed in it strange and even heretical.

Not only in language, but also in thought, Ecclesiastes is unique in the Old Testament. It consists of the reflections of a sage who could find little of man in human life. Wherever he looked in the world of man or of physical nature, he saw futility and aimless existence. His constant refrain is the well-known " Vanity of vanities; all is vanity." Neither right nor wrong makes any difference to the fate of man; he gains nothing by the former and loses nothing by the latter, for both paths lead only to death. He has heard, it seems, of a doctrine which tells of another life, but finds no evidence for it.

At the same time, the writer adopts what looks like an inconsistent attitude to religion and ethics. He holds strongly that God is the supreme ruler of the universe, and controls the fate of men. Men will do well to make the best of the life they have, but must not forget the divine ruler of the world, and that best can be attained only by upright conduct.

While, then, the book is, in a sense, one of the most pessimistic in general literature, it has its lessons. In Jewish thought even so hopeless an outlook as that of its writer still involved a stern devotion to the will of God.

Lamentations. One characteristic type in ancient Jewish literature is the dirge. Originally an improvised utterance sung at a funeral, it was extended to other purposes. In Amos, for example, we have a dirge to be sung over Israel, which is depicted as a dead virgin (Am. v, 2). In this book we have five such poems. The first four are alphabetic acrostics; the fifth looks as though it might have been modified into such a form, as it has twenty-two verses. Each has its own distinctive character, and it seems clear that they come from several different authors and were composed under different conditions. It is interesting to note that in chs. ii-iv there is a slight variation from the usual order of the Hebrew alphabet, the letters called Ayin and Pe being transposed.

The first dirge has three lines to each letter, but only the first begins with it. It is a lament over the desolate condition of Jerusalem after the calamity of 586 B.C. But we get the impression that some time has elapsed since the fall of the city; the tone is rather that of a dull and hopeless ache than of the sudden agony of disaster. It is the plight of the ruined city rather than the horror of the sack which oppresses the poet.

In structure the second poem resembles the first, except for the alphabetic change already noted. Here, too, the situation is different. It is the actual sack of Jerusalem, with the sufferings of the siege itself which is brought before our eyes. It stands on a higher level as literature than ch. i, magnificent as that poem is. But ch. ii is one of the most moving pieces of poetry which have come down to us from the ancient world.

Ch. iii also contains three lines to the letter, but here each line begins with the significant letter. We thus have in our Bibles sixty-six verses, though the three poems in chs. i-iii are of the same length. The literary standard again is not so high as in the first two chapters, but it still remains a poem of great beauty. Even more than in ch. i we feel that the actual sack of Jerusalem is a thing of the past, though its results remain, and the land is still desolate.

In ch. iv we are back once more in the atmosphere of ch. ii. Indeed, some scholars think that these two poems are the work of the same author. Here, however, we have only two lines to each letter, which occurs only at the beginning of the first and not at that of the second.

All four of these poems are written in a 3:2 (with occasional 2:2) "metre." It was, indeed, first recognised in this book, and is often called the "Qinah" or "dirge" metre. It seems peculiarly suited to such poems, though it is by no means confined to them; it is, for example, the metre of Ps. xxiii.

The fifth poem is hardly a dirge. It contains only twenty-two lines, and the "metre" is 3:3. It is rather a prayer uttered by one in deep suffering, which is not necessarily that of the beseiged and ruined city. There are references to famine and to enemies, but such may be found elsewhere; the poem is not so closely connected with the destruction of Jerusalem by Nebuchadrezzar as are the others.

The authorship of these poems is quite uncertain. Tradition ascribed them to Jeremiah, who is said to have written a dirge on Josiah which, with other poems on the same subject, was included in the book of Lamentations (II Chron. xxxv, 25). But none of these poems refers specifically to Josiah. A king is mentioned in iv, 20, but this is almost certainly Zedekiah, and the terms used would hardly have been applied to him by Jeremiah. We may, however, be reasonably sure that chs. i, ii and iv came from the lifetime of Jeremiah. Of these ii and iv must have been composed very shortly after the fall of the city, ch. i a little later, but still in the early days of the exile, and ch. iii later still, though this also is earlier than the restoration. We have no clue as to the date of ch. v.

Esther.   This is clearly one of the latest books in the Old Testament. It claims to record events which took place in the reign of Xerxes, the famous Persian king who failed to conquer Greece. At the earliest, then, it must come from the fifth century, and scholars are inclined to regard it as a romantic story intended to encourage the Jews in a time of persecution, probably dating from the Maccabaean period in the middle of the second century B.C. It is curious to find that the names given to the prominent Jewish characters are suggestive of Babylonian deities; Esther looks very like Ishtar, the great fertility goddess of western Asia, and it is difficult not to find a verbal connection between Mordecai and Marduk, the patron god of Babylon. One other peculiarity is that the divine name

Yahweh does not occur in it; for this reason it is freely copied, and comparatively little care is taken to see that it does not fall into profane hands.

The story is well known. The king (his name in Persian is Khshayarsha, pronounced by the Greeks Xerxes and by the Jews Ahasuerus) was displeased by the behaviour of his queen Vashti, and deposed her. In her place he selected a Jewish girl named Esther, whose uncle, Mordecai, was about the royal court, though the fact was not disclosed. Mordecai was able to discover and frustrate a plot against the king's life, but received no special reward for his services.

A certain Haman became the king's favourite, and received extraordinary honours. The whole court showed him peculiar respect, with the exception of Mordecai, who refused to bow before him. To take revenge on Mordecai, Haman secured a royal edict ordering the destruction of all Jews in the Persian empire on a date some eleven months after the decree was issued.

Mordecai appealed to Esther, who came to the king, and asked that she might entertain him and Haman at a banquet. At its close she invited them to come again the following night. Delighted with this new honour, Haman prepared a "gallows," or rather a tree on which Mordecai might be impaled. But in the night, the king was unable to sleep, and heard read the story of the plot which Mordecai had exposed. In the morning he compelled Haman to arrange for a ceremonial procession in which honour should be given to Mordecai.

At that evening's banquet Esther told the king that Haman was plotting to destroy her and all her people. In his anger, the king had Haman executed on the " gallows " he had prepared for Mordecai, gave Mordecai the favourite position, and issued a second decree authorising all Jews to defend themselves on the appointed day, and calling on all officials to help them against their enemies. Ever afterwards the Jews celebrated their escape in a special festival called Purim, observed on the fourteenth and fifteenth days of the month Adar.

The book seems to have a double purpose; on the one hand it illustrates God's care of His people, and the vengeance He would take on their enemies, and on the other it explains the origin of the feast of Purim.

CHAPTER XX

THE WRITINGS: DANIEL

THE Book of Daniel was not included among the Prophets by Palestinian Jews. In the Egyptian tradition, however, it is normally placed after Ezekiel, and this position has been adopted by the Christian Church, since it was accepted by New Testament writers. In Palestine it seems to have been unknown at the beginning of the second century B.C. A similar but not identical name is found in Ezekiel (xiv, 14, 20, xxviii, 3), but there is no mention here of a book by this person, and it seems that there has been some confusion with a traditional Semitic hero whose existence has recently become known to us.

The book falls into two parts. The first, comprising chs. i-vi, contains narratives concerning Daniel, a young man who was taken to Babylon with Jehoiachin, and reached a high position at court. This he retained after the conquest of Babylon by the Persians, though no event is ascribed to the reign of either of the first two Persian kings. The second part of the book consists of apocalyptic visions, which purport to predict accurately events which took place in the first part of the second century B.C. Historians regard this section as an original and most important document for this period.

There is a further distinction between two parts of the book. From ii, 4 to the end of ch. vii the language used is Aramaic; in the rest of the book it is Hebrew. The Aramaic is of a type which appears to be not earlier than the early part of the fourth century B.C., and may be two centuries later.

The general impression made by the book as a whole is that it reached its present form during the reign of Antiochus Epiphanes, roughly between 180 and 160 B.C. It would then be the work of a writer who wished to encourage his fellow Jews to resist the tyrant's efforts to root out the Jewish faith. The stories in the first section, however, look as though they were earlier; they generally end with the conversion of the king, and Jews of the Maccabaean age would surely rather that Antiochus had died in his sins. Further, it is difficult to reconcile some of the statements in these chapters with what is definitely known of the period. Belshazzar, son of the last king of Babylon, Nabunaid, never formally ascended the throne, though he was left in charge of Babylon during the last years of its empire. He was killed, it appears, at the battle of Opis, some hundred and fifty miles north of Babylon, and Cyrus entered the capital peacefully. Indeed, he claims that he came as a deliverer and not as a conqueror. Moreover, the Book of Daniel interposes a Persian king named Darius the Mede between Nabunaid (or Belshazzar) and Cyrus. The first Darius mentioned in contemporary annals is Darius Hystapes, who succeeded Cambyses, the son of Cyrus, in 522 B.C., after a period of confusion. And in other points the references in the Book of Daniel differ from what is actually known of the age in a way which makes it very difficult to believe that the stories reached their present form in the sixth century B.C.

The language question raises serious difficulties which have never been wholly removed. If the Hebrew had been resumed at the beginning of ch. vii, it would be easy to suppose that the stories of chs. ii-vi had been written in Aramaic originally, and were simply copied in that language. But ch. vii, which is also in Aramaic, belongs to the apocalyptic section. If the book, in its present form, is the work of a single author, as many scholars believe it to be, then we must suppose that the change from Hebrew to Aramaic and back again to Hebrew, was due to reasons which we can no longer ascertain. It has also been suggested that the Aramaic was translated from an original Hebrew, but that leaves unanswered the question, Why did the translator not begin at the beginning and go on to the end? The best suggestion yet made is that the author began to write in Hebrew, then at ii, 4 changed to Aramaic, intending to complete the book in that language, but when he reached the end of ch. vii realised that Hebrew was better suited to his purpose; it was still in use as a literary language at the beginning of the first century B.C.

The contents of the book are as follows :

A. Chs. i-vi. The narratives.

i. Daniel, with three other noble youths, is taken as a prisoner by Nebuchadnezzar to Babylon. There he is trained as an astrologer, but refuses to eat food that, from the Jewish point of view, was defiled by heathen contact. He is allowed to experiment with simple and harmless food, and is successful. These four become the wisest of their time.

ii. Nebuchadnezzar had a dream in which he sees a great image composed of various materials. He demands of his astrologers that they should interpret the dream, but in order to assure himself that their interpretation is reliable, orders them first to tell him the dream. If they can do this, he will know that they are competent to offer an interpretation. They protest that this is the wrong way to do things, and they cannot be expected to interpret a dream unless it is described to them. The king orders them all to be killed, but Daniel intercedes in time and secures a reprieve. He then describes the dream correctly to the king, and gives the interpretation. The king raises him to high honour.

iii. (Daniel is not mentioned in this story). Nebuchadnezzar sets up a great image, and demands that all his people shall worship it. Daniel's three companions refuse and are thrown into a blazing furnace. There, however, they are miraculously preserved, and when the king looks into the furnace he sees them walking about unharmed. With them is a fourth figure in human form. He brings them out and recognises that their God is the only deity fit to be worshipped. He makes a decree forbidding, under pain of death, any criticism or adverse remark on the God of Israel.

iv. Nebuchadnezzar has another dream. Daniel interprets this as indicating that for a time madness will fall on the king, and he will be driven out from human society. In a moment of great pride, the doom falls upon him, and he becomes as a beast. On his recovery he acknowledges the supremacy of the Most High God.

v. King Belshazzar makes a great feast to his chief officers. He calls for the sacred vessels which had been brought from the temple at Jerusalem, that he and his guests may drink from them. At that moment a hand appears, writing on the wall. None can read this till Daniel is brought in. He identifies the words as being three Aramaic terms, normally used for coins, a Mina, a Shekel, and some small change. But Daniel interprets these as indicating that Belshazzar has been weighed in the balances and found wanting, and that his kingdom will be divided and given to the Medes and Persians. That night Belshazzar is killed, and Darius the Mede becomes king.

vi. Darius is now king. He makes a decree that any person in his dominions who appeals to man or god other than himself shall be thrown into a den of lions. Daniel still continues to pray to the God of Israel, with his face to Jerusalem. This is reported to the king, who, most unwillingly, has to see the sentence carried out. But the lions do Daniel no harm, and in the morning the king finds him quite safe. His accusers are then thrown into the pit, and are killed before they can reach the ground. Darius then circulates a rescript through his dominions, recording the event and calling on all nations to praise the God of Daniel.

B. The visions.

vii. In the first year of Belshazzar's reign, Daniel sees in a vision four beasts, and from the fourth spring ten horns. One of these horns is particularly strong and violent, seeking to destroy the saints. But thrones are set and an " ancient of days " takes his place. The great beast is slain, and one in human form comes up to the ancient of days and receives from him dominion over all the earth. An angel gives Daniel the interpretation. The beasts are kingdoms, and the horns are kings. Upon them, and especially on the " little " horn, judgment will come and God's representative shall be established over all mankind.

This is typical apocalypse. First, history in the guise of parable. The identity of the four kingdoms is much discussed, and various identifications have been proposed. The most probable seems to be that they are the four kingdoms into which the empire of Alexander the Great was divided. The little horn will then be Antiochus Epiphanes, and at this point history gives way to eschatology. That is the date at which a work was composed in normal eschatological writing, and the date accepted for this book by most modern scholars.

viii. In the third year of Belshazzar, Daniel has another vision. First appears an aggressive ram, which made conquests in every direction. Then comes a he-goat, which overthrows the ram. Its horn, however, is soon broken, and four others appear. From one of these four there sprang a little horn, which in turn grew strong, and attacked Judah, destroying the sanctuary of God.

The explanation is fairly obvious, and is confirmed by the divine interpreter. The ram is the Medo-Persian empire. The he-goat is Alexander the Great, and the four horns are the four kingdoms into which his empire was divided. The little horn is once more Antiochus Epiphanes. Here the language is definitely eschatological, for these things are to happen " at the end " (v. 19).

ix. In the first year of Darius (here called the son of Xerxes), Daniel tries to solve the meaning of the " seventy years " during which Jeremiah had prophesied that the exile should last (Jer. xxix, 10). He is told that these " years " are really " weeks of years," which would make the total period four hundred and ninety years. If we can assume that the writer does not regard the liberation of Judah as being complete till the restoration of temple worship in 164 B.C. this figure is only fifty or sixty years out, for Jeremiah's prediction is probably somewhere about 592 B.C. At the end of the first seven weeks the temple is to be rebuilt. Sixty-two weeks later further trouble is to come; the " Anointed " will be killed, and the city and sanctuary ruined. Finally, the oppressor will make a covenant for many during the last " week," and for half that time sacrifice and offering will cease.

Though the figures do not fit the earlier periods, they are fairly accurate in this last period if the reference is to Antiochus Epiphanes. There was a strong body of Jews who accepted his views and were prepared to support him. It was only with the outbreak of the Maccabaean revolt in 167 that an effort was made to resist this heathen aggression. The period between this and the resumption of sacrifice was not quite three and a half years, but it was over three.

x-xi, dated in the third year of Cyrus, give a fairly accurate account of political and military movements in the period preceding the reign of Antiochus Epiphanes, especially the struggle between the Seleucids and the Ptolemies for the possession of Palestine, which had once more become a " buffer state " between the great Asiatic and African powers. Towards the end of ch. xi we have another account of the reign of Antiochus, and the chapter concludes with his death.

xii. The Messianic age is inaugurated in vv. 1-3. In v. 2 we have one of the very few clear references to a valid life after death in the Old Testament. Even here the resurrection is not universal; " many," not " all " shall awake from their sleep in the dust. Finally " two others " are seen standing one on each side of a river, and Daniel is given the date at which the end shall come. It is either 1290 or 1235 days after the cessation of sacrifice in the temple. This is between three and four years, and may be taken as indicating again the period during which the temple remained defiled. Clearly the writer expected the consummation of the age in the near future.

The Book of Daniel has had an enormous influence on later religious thinking. It is one of the earliest great Apocalypses of which we have so many specimens down to the second century A.D., and it set the tone for them all. It went far to shape the eschatological ideas current in Palestine in the time of our Lord, and we meet constant reminiscences of it in the great Christian Apocalypse which stands at the end of our New Testament. There are still only adumbrations of Messianic teaching, which pursued a line independent of eschatology for some centuries, and seems to have been united to it only in the first century B.C. It is to be noted that even in xii, 1 the great eschatological figure is not " the Anointed," but the " great Prince Michael," always recognised as an archangel in Jewish and Christian theology, but seldom if ever as the Messiah.

Like all Scripture, this book was written with the purpose of bringing home to its immediate audience certain truths which are eternally valid. It is for us who follow so many centuries after their time to isolate the truth from its temporal and racial surroundings, and to adapt it to ourselves and our own day.

CHAPTER XXI

THE WRITINGS: EZRA, NEHEMIAH, CHRONICLES

It seems almost certain that the last three books in the Hebrew Bible really form a single work. They are no longer in their original order, which may be due to the fact that while Ezra and Nehemiah added something to the history given in Kings, Chronicles covered the same ground as the earlier book. But the last verses of Chronicles are identical with the opening of Ezra, and the same style and general outlook are manifest throughout the three books. Except where Chronicles is quoting directly from older works, the language in which it is written is a Hebrew which shows signs of change from the classical type, though it is far from reaching the form which we find in Ecclesiastes. In Ezra we find a certain amount of Aramaic, mainly copies of official documents, though in v. 1-5 we find a short narrative linking two of these together.

There are several indications of the date at which this long work was composed. In I Chron. iii, 10-24 we have the genealogy of David's descendants; it is carried down for six generations after Zerubbabel, that is well into the fourth century B.C. Again, in Neh. xii, 22 a priest named Jaddua is mentioned, and we know that he was a contemporary of Alexander the Great. The work, then, cannot have reached its final form till the fourth century.

The purpose of the writer, or rather the compiler, is clear. He gives us the history of Judah from a priestly point of view. He is not greatly interested in northern Israel, except where it is in some way connected with Judah. For him the centre of the world is the temple, and that is in Jerusalem and belongs to Judah. He has a great deal of information to give us about details of the temple worship and the organisation of the priesthood. From time to time, too, he draws a moral or adds incidents which illustrate his religious principles. Thus he tells us why Uzziah was struck with leprosy (II Chron. xxvi, 16-20), adds to the misfortunes of Ahaz (II Chron. xxviii, 18, 19), and records the repentance of Manasseh (II Chron. xxxiii, 11-16). In dealing with the reign of Abijah he omits the condemnation passed on the king in I Kings xv, 3, and records a victory over Jeroboam. Clearly what matters is not the triumph of Abijah, but the defeat of Jeroboam. Successes are ascribed also to the good kings, Asa and Jehoshaphat.

How much of this rested on actual documents, and how much is tradition worked up to suit the writer's purpose, it is impossible to say. He probably had some more or less reliable account of Josiah's death for he would hardly have ascribed to so good a king the disregard of divine injunctions which proved fatal (II Chron. xxxv, 22). Further, he gives an account of a battle for which there is no room in the narrative of II Kings xxiii, 29, 30.

Some of the sources on which the compiler of Chronicles relied are fairly clear. He had before him all our Old Testament books from Genesis to II Kings, with the possible exception of Ruth. He had also genealogical lists which had been carefully kept, especially in the priestly families. It is to be noted that these went back to the days of the monarchy, and it is a matter of surprise that they survived the period of the exile. They must have been preserved by men like Ezekiel, who came of priestly stock, and carried with them a few of the records. Temple archives, too, seem to have been at the disposal of the compiler, though, again, it is not clear how they could have come into his hands.

Chronicles is, then, a revision of earlier writings. But in Ezra and Nehemiah the compiler is dealing with events for which the older historical works provided no documents. He knew of the prophecies uttered by Haggai and Zechariah, but his other sources have not, in the main, come down to us. He does, however, quote *verbatim* important official despatches to and from the Persian court, preserving them in the original Aramaic (Ezr. iv, 8-23, v. 6-vi, 12, vii, 12-26).

It is also clear that the compiler was able to use memoirs of both Ezra and Nehemiah. The latter is a particularly interesting character; he has energy and faith, and deals vigorously with all who oppose him, whether they are Jews or foreigners. In other places they are mentioned in the third person, but here also it seems probable that the compiler was relying on documents contemporary with the events he describes.

II Chronicles ends and Ezra begins with a decree issued by Cyrus immediately after his occupation of Babylon, ordering the restoration of the temple at Jerusalem, and giving permission to Jews to return to Palestine if they so desired. A party went out under a certain Sheshbazzar, of whom we hear no more. The attempt to reorganise the national life of Judah round the restored temple seems to have been abortive, and, apparently few Jews availed themselves of the opportunity offered to them. At the beginning of Ezra ii we hear of Zerubbabel, a grandson of Jehoiachin, as the leader of the people in Jerusalem. An altar is set up, but no attempt is made to rebuild the temple itself till 520, eighteen years after the original decree of Cyrus. The delay is due to the jealousy of the governors and people of Samaria, which continued to be a separate province as it had been under Assyrian and Babylonian government.

Once started, however, the building of the temple continued, and was completed in 516 B.C. Then follow some correspondence between the local governors and the court of Persia. One letter is addressed to Xerxes (Ezra iv, 6) and one to Artaxerxes (iv, 7*ff*.); the latter is given in full. This, however, does not refer to the temple, but to the rebuilding of the walls of Jerusalem. Since the earliest possible date for this is 464 B.C., it would seem to be out of place here.

We then (v. i) go back to the reign of Darius, and hear that the temple is rebuilt. There is further correspondence with the court, the original decree of Cyrus is discovered, and the local governors are ordered to help and not to hinder.

A gap of at least sixty years (possibly twice as long) follows, and Ezra comes to Jerusalem, and inaugurates a reform which begins with the dissolution of all " mixed " marriages. In the twentieth year of Artaxerxes' reign (444 B.C.) Nehemiah becomes governor, and sets about the building of the city wall. He has to face opposition from other local governors, but succeeds in spite of them. At this point there is no reference to an appeal to the Persian court, but the correspondence already mentioned in Ezra iv, 7*ff*. may belong to this period. If that is so, then Nehemiah worked too fast to allow any royal prohibition to interfere with his work, and the wall was finished in fifty-two days.

In Neh. viii, 1 a solemn assembly was held at which Ezra read the Law, and the remainder of the book is chiefly occupied with measures taken by Nehemiah to carry out its injunctions. There was an interval in his governorship, for he was recalled to Babylon in the thirty-second year of Artaxerxes, though he returned " after certain days."

In recent years doubts have arisen as to the order of the events described in Ezra-Nehemiah. We have seen that the compiler's sense of chronology was imperfect, and today there is a strong impression in many quarters that Ezra and Nehemiah were not strictly contemporaries. Dates are given by the regnal years of King Artaxerxes. But there were three kings of that name, and it is not clear that we can justify the old assumption that Artaxerxes I (came to the throne in 464 B.C.) is always the man intended. Artaxerxes III is out of the question; his reign was too short. But Artaxerxes II (came to the throne in 404 B.C.) and had a long reign. Ezra and Nehemiah are only once mentioned together (Neh. xii, 26), though Neh. x, 1 might be taken to imply that they were contemporaries, since Nehemiah is sealed with others after the great act of penitence and confession recorded in ch. ix. This, however, might be explained in other ways, and there is a growing feeling that while Nehemiah is to be dated in the reign of Artaxerxes I, Ezra belongs to that of Artaxerxes II, and therefore began his work at Jerusalem, not in 458 B.C. but in 398.

This question, however, is of minor importance, for, in whatever order they came, the work of these two men was a turning point in the history of Israel. It was they, more than any others, who sketched the pattern of Judaism, with its genuine piety, its devotion to the Law, and its exclusiveness. We have no direct information as to the state of Judah between Zerubbabel and Nehemiah, but we have a number of documents from a Jewish settlement at Elephantine, far up the Nile; they are dated in the fifth century B.C. These people had a temple to Yahweh, whom they regarded as their chief God, but it is clear that their religion was much mixed with other elements, derived, apparently from Palestine and not from Egypt. Other deities were associated with Yahweh, and these Jews seem to have had no suspicion that there was anything wrong. It is at least possible that Judah might have drifted into a similar mixed faith, and it is certain that, but for the work of Nehemiah and Ezra, the Jews would never have developed that passionate reverence for the Law and the temple which enabled them to resist the proselytising (to use a mild term) of Antiochus Epiphanes. In that case, the only pure monotheism known on earth would have perished, and the first requisite of the Christian revelation would have had no meaning for any people in the world.

BIBLIOGRAPHY

Some introduction to each book of the Old Testament will be found in every good commentary. Of the one-volume commentaries on the whole Bible the following may be mentioned:

Teachers' Commentary. S.C.M. Press. 15s.

A New Commentary on Holy Scripture. Ed. Gore. S.P.C.K.
31s. 6d.

A Concise Bible Commentary. Ed. W. K. Lowther Clarke.
S.P.C.K. 30s.

A Catholic Commentary on Holy Scripture. Nelson. 84s.

There are several series of commentaries, which, naturally, vary a good deal with different contributors; prices also usually differ in the different volumes. The following may be mentioned:

The International Critical Commentary. T. & T. Clark.

The Westminster Commentaries. Methuen.

Both these are suitable for advanced students; the former, though useful to all readers, can be fully appreciated only by those who have some knowledge of Hebrew.

The Revised Version for Schools. C.U.P. 3s. 6d. each.

The Cambridge Bible for Schools. C.U.P.

The Clarendon Bible for Schools. O.U.P. The Old Testament volumes include only selections from the various books.

The Century Bible. T. C. & E. C. Jack.

An outstanding volume on a single book (Jeremiah) is *Prophecy and Religion.* J. Skinner. C.U.P. 21s.

The following books deal with the Old Testament in general:

The Holy Bible: Revised Standard Version. Nelson. 30s.

A Companion to the Bible. Ed. T. W. Manson.
T. & T. Clark. 16s.

A Guide-Book to the Bible. A. Parmelee. E.U.P. 6s.

The Old Testament. T. H. Robinson, E. Arnold. 3s. 6d. (Merlin Books, especially suitable for beginners.)

Israel. J. Pedersen. O.U.P., 2 vols.; Vol. I 28s., Vol. II 45s.

A New Approach to the Old Testament. A. C. Alington.
Bell. 6s.

The Meaning of the Old Testament. H. Martin. S.C.M. Press.
3s. 6d.

The Bible Today. C. H. Dodd. C.U.P. 6s.

The Authority of the Old Testament. A. G. Hebert.
Faber. 16s.

The Bible from Within. A. G. Hebert. O.U.P. 8s. 6d.

For the history of the Old Testament Text one book is indispensable:

The Old Testament Text and Version. B. J. Roberts.
University of Wales Press. 21s.

The following deal with the individual books of the Old Testament:

Introduction to the Old Testament. A. Bentzen.
G. E. C. Gad, Copenhagen.

An Introduction to the Books of the Old Testament.
W. O. E. Oesterley and T. H. Robinson. S.P.C.K.

A Short Introduction to the Old Testament. I. Allen.
O.U.P. 2s. 6d.

The Old Testament, its Making and Meaning. H. Wheeler
Robinson. London University Press. 7s. 6d.

The Growth of the Old Testament. H. H. Rowley.
Hutchinson. 8s. 6d.

Pentateuchal Criticism. D. C. Simpson. O.U.P. 6s. 6d.

Prophecy and the Prophets in Ancient Israel.
T. H. Robinson. Duckworth. 8s. 6d.

The Poetry of the Old Testament. T. H. Robinson.
Duckworth. 8s. 6d.

On Old Testament History the following may be consulted:

Historical Geography of the Holy Land. G. A. Smith, T. & T.
Clark. (Indispensable O.P., but second-hand copies are sometimes to be had.)

The History of Israel. W. O. E. Oesterley and T. H. Robinson.
2 vols. O.U.P. 21s. each.

The History of Israel. H. Wheeler Robinson. Duckworth. 8s. 6d.

Among the many books on the Religion of Israel the following may be noted:

A Theological Word-Book of the Bible. Ed. A. Richardson.
S.C.M. Press. 25s.

Religious Ideas of the Old Testament. H. Wheeler Robinson.
Duckworth. 8s. 6d.

Hebrew Religion. W. O. E. Oesterley and T. H. Robinson.
S.P.C.K. 14s. 6d.

Further information may be derived from the Institute of Christian Education, 46 Gordon Square, London, W.C.1.